The 90% Solution

A Consistent Approach to Optimal Business Decisions

by

Thomas P. McAuliffe

First published by AuthorHouse 08/29/05

ISBN: 1-4208-4621-3 (sc)

Library of Congress Control Number: 2005903209

Printed in the United States of America
Bloomington, Indiana

This book is printed on acid-free paper.

author HOUSE

1663 LIBERTY DRIVE
BLOOMINGTON, INDIANA 47403
(800) 839-8640
www.authorhouse.com

Nothing is more difficult, and therefore more precious,
than to be able to decide.

—Napoleon Bonaparte

ACKNOWLEDGEMENTS

I would like to extend very special thanks to Donald G. Hanson, Ph.D. and Carolyn S. Shamlin for an excellent job of editing this work. Anyone who has ever written a book knows how important editors and supportive friends are to the tedious process of refining sentence structure, punctuation, and message. In a busy world, they somehow found the extra time to support my efforts and were brilliant contributors to the quality of this project.

I would also like to thank several business associates and mentors from my formative years at General Electric who showed everyone the values of integrity, mutual respect, and strength under pressure. A short list of these *bright lights* would include Walt Williams (to whom this book is dedicated), Charlie Gustafson, Bill Bierenkoven, John Karcanes, Claude Frederick, and Tom Macmanus.

Finally, I would to thank Jack Welch for creating an entrepreneurial environment that always rewarded bold thinking and made anything seem possible. Within this structure, everyone was encouraged to aim high and to be successful. It was an adventure to be there.

DEDICATION

This book is dedicated to Walter W. Williams. A true friend and one of the finest executives I have ever met. Walt grew up in a small town and a modest home with six brothers and sisters. After high school and service in the U.S. Marine Corps, he joined the General Electric Company as an hourly worker in the warehouse in Utica, New York.

From there he grew to become the only person in GE history to start in the warehouse and end up a senior vice president. He was highly regarded by everyone who worked with or for him along the way. Walt was positive in the worst of circumstances and had a way of making even difficult businesses seem fun. He was respectful of everyone: no one had to leave their dignity behind after one of his meetings. Find a better model for leadership if you can.

Walt went on to become chairman and CEO of Rubbermaid. He managed this meteoric rise while having four children, and almost always made it home in time to have dinner with his family. Not many high-level executives can make this statement.

His meetings were so well-organized and focused that he always accomplished more than his peers, who normally toiled well into the evening. He was a truly great *decision-maker* and could work through issues faster than any of his contemporaries while achieving excellent results.

Walt's whole life has been a series of one good decision (business and personal) after another. This book is dedicated to him in the hope that some of you might do so well with your own lives.

Thanks for showing the way, Walter—you are one of the very best.

TABLE OF CONTENTS

ACKNOWLEDGEMENTS v

DEDICATION.. vii

TABLE OF CONTENTS.. ix

INTRODUCTION 1

Chapter I	FUNDAMENTAL DISTINCTIONS	5
Chapter II	COMMON APPROACHES	7
Chapter III	THE NEED FOR A BETTER PROCESS	9
Chapter IV	RECOGNIZING A SIGNIFICANT DECISION	11
Chapter V	BUILDING A DECISION MATRIX	15
Chapter VI	CRITERIA COMPRESSION	33
Chapter VII	CREATIVE ALTERNATIVES	41
Chapter VIII	SEQUENTIAL DECISIONS	53
Chapter IX	TESTING FOR INTRINSIC MERIT	63
Chapter X	GROUP DECISION-MAKING	75
Chapter XI	SELLING YOUR DECISIONS	87
Chapter XII	THE DECISIVE MANAGEMENT CULTURE	93
Appendix A	Instructions—Using a Matrix Library	97
Appendix B	Instructions—Decision Matrix Basics	99
Appendix C	Advanced Techniques & Reminders	103
Appendix D	Decision Worksheets	107

INTRODUCTION

The process offered in this book started one day very early in my career thirty-five years ago. As a young MBA surrounded by one hundred other young managers and managers-to-be, I was sitting in class at a remote place on the Hudson River known as *Crotonville*. This is the corporate training facility now known as the John F. Welch Leadership Center. It represents the core of a $1 billion per year General Electric effort to educate and expand the thinking of managers and executives at all levels.

I remember learning the fundamentals of objective decision-making while writing extensively in the margins of my notepad. One of my co-workers became curious and leaned over to ask what all my notes were about. I told him I thought I already had a good use for this process and was excited about its potential for sorting out new product designs. At the time, I was a product planner for a small product line and was already thinking about a basic design choice that was awaiting my return to the *real world* after the training session at Crotonville.

At the end of an intense week of courses, I returned on a Sunday and went to my office to catch up on mail. When I entered my small office, I found it papered wall-to-wall with about twenty-five concept renderings from the industrial design group. Amidst the chaos, there was a note from my boss saying that he, along with three senior product planners, had spent four hours arguing the pros and cons of each concept and had narrowed the choice to five favorites for me to consider.

I ignored the note and their choices all together. In fact, I ignored all of the renderings until I retrieved my set of "objectives" scribbled during the training session. I thought why not try the process now? I would see how it worked in a real situation and where it would lead. In ten minutes, I had it down to three choices (none of which was in the group of five chosen for me). In another fifteen minutes, I had a final choice and one in which I had great confidence. I left the office with a high level of enthusiasm for my design choice and a new business weapon—a way to make smart decisions fast.

Normally it would have taken another few hours to convince others of my decision. My immediate superior was a very contentious and difficult human being. His positions would also be bolstered by the opinions of those he had assembled for design review. When I presented my one-page summary the next day, the session was over in five minutes—there was no argument. I learned another lesson about a good decision-making process—it can also be used to "sell" your point of view, even to a biased or stubborn audience.

It was the beginning of an evolution that continued through four companies and thousands of decisions. As I grew, so did the process. I used this evolving process for every important decision along the way and didn't make many mistakes. By the time I left for the entrepreneurial world, I had become the leading product manager and one of the top-rated executives in the consumer sector—about one third of GE at the time. This story is not intended to extol the highlights of my career but rather to send the message that very good decisions are important to success and years of good decisions can define a career.

If there was a "turning point" in my career, it happened on that day. There would have been no way for me to imagine how this basic idea would grow in nature and substance or how widely it could be applied with great effectiveness. What started out as a personal process to compare product design alternatives, became a sophisticated but simple way to approach all important decisions across a broad spectrum; career path alternatives, key personnel decisions, competitive strategy choices, pricing solutions, profit optimization approaches, merger and acquisition candidates, and any other decision of consequence. It also became the most efficient way to communicate and sell my decisions.

The process described in this book bears little resemblance to the notes I made that day. It still retains the advantages of speed and flexibility but has been expanded and refined by pragmatic use into a powerful tool that any reader can learn quickly and use effectively. The process also offers something that I have not found in any other decision technique—a way to determine if the best alternative is *good enough*. There is no gain in choosing the best among a group of alternatives if that choice is not going to measure up. *The pick of the litter might not turn out to be a great dog.*

It is the combination of sorting out the best alternative, and then holding it to a corporate standard for excellence, that can change a career or an entire business culture with consistently better results.

Note: all of the examples used in this book are derived from real business situations in a variety of companies; from manufacturing to software, from low-tech to high, from small to the very large. The cases come from direct experience within a variety of companies as a manager or corporate leader, and as a consultant or external observer. The exact details have been modified where necessary to protect confidential information and specific individuals. I think you will find them applicable to your business no matter the size of your entity or the specific nature of your industry. Management decisions are universal.

Chapter I

FUNDAMENTAL DISTINCTIONS

Management decisions are discussed widely in hundreds of books and articles by experts of all types. The philosophies range from quantitative methods to spiritual reflection. Some are overly simplistic while others are highly complex and theoretical. With all due respect to differing approaches and with an admission of personal bias, I have not found any that would be practical as the core of an effective management process. This book is an attempt to create something quite different: a consistent approach that can be used and understood by any manager or management team facing significant decisions. In order to begin in a productive manner, it is necessary to grasp two fundamental distinctions.

Problems and decisions. A problem occurs when some element of your business is not working satisfactorily. Some part of the process has changed or is malfunctioning and you don't know what it is or why. For example, your sales cycle is growing longer and revenues are slipping. It may be the market changing, competitive actions, the aging of your product line, ineffective pricing or merchandising programs, deteriorating sales team performance, or something else. Solving the problem requires an *analysis* of all relevant dynamics. The *decision* about what to do to fix the problem comes later—after the problem is fully understood. At that point, alternative solutions can be considered and the best of these adopted. If analysis of the problem determines that it is a failure of sales management at the top of the structure, then new a vice president of sales may be the answer. Choosing a new VP of sales would be an important "decision." It should not be thought of as a "problem."

The process for understanding a puzzle is completely different from the process of choosing among alternative solutions. Do not mix these two or your efforts are not likely to produce good results. If you were racing a small sailboat and noticed that you were no longer going as fast as your chief competitors, you might want to evaluate sail trim, boat balance, centerboard positioning, wind and current differences, and other possible causes. Choosing a different set of sails will not help you if you just needed to remove the seaweed from your rudder.

Analysts and managers. Analysts are specially-trained individuals who are skilled in the use of analytical tools and processes. Their general role is one of support to the decision-making process. Their greatest assets are time, specialization, and the ability to contribute knowledge. In doing so, they may employ a wide range of quantitative tools from simple spreadsheets to more complicated methods like linear programming or Monte Carlo simulations. It is important to understand that output from these models does not provide *decisions*, but rather inputs to decisions.

Managers are rarely skilled in the use of sophisticated models—the time necessary to become proficient and to use these tools would be a poor investment. The primary role of management is the use of knowledge to direct resources, rather than the generation of basic knowledge. Their greatest assets are vision, judgment, energy, and organization skills. Their scarcest resource is time. The *decision matrix concept* presented in this book is a process tool designed solely for managers. It is fundamentally different from the models and tools used by analysts but can easily incorporate qualitative and quantitative inputs from any source.

Chapter II

COMMON APPROACHES

Instinct. I know many of you will be offended, but some of the worst decision-makers I have ever met rely primarily on instinct, intuition, or *gut feel* to make decisions. Even some very smart people give this out to others as good advice. Most of the time, this is very bad advice. How many smart people do you know who have made terrible *life decisions* based on intuition alone? The same patterns hold true for business. I know many such people and many are in high places. This book is for those people too.

The fundamental weakness in the instinctive approach is that it collapses all thoughts, emotions, objectives, conflicting elements, and risks into one consideration—how you *feel* about one choice versus another. This is the *emotional approach* to decision-making. If you address complex or difficult decisions in this manner, you are likely to swim in circles, make poor choices, struggle to remember why you made the choices you did, or end up making no choices at all. Intuition has a place in every big decision, but there is a better way to use it—as a part of a process, rather than as *the process* itself.

In addition, it may be the worst possible approach if you have to justify or explain your decisions to others—especially going up the chain of command. If your decisions are always accepted by your superiors, this may work for you. If, however, your decisions are challenged—as is more often the case—explaining that your choices just "felt right" to you will be the weakest possible justification. If you have to "sell" your decisions over and over again, it is an indication that you have made an *emotional case* rather than a *rational case.*

However, there are good elements packaged in what we call instinct or intuition and these can be beneficial. As every decision will contain qualitative aspects and subjective projections, intuition will always play an important role. In a positive sense, intuition and instinct contain experience, wisdom, and judgment, and all of these should be put to productive use—you just need to learn how to break them down into their component parts.

Plus and minus. Each of you probably knows how this works. The first step is to attempt to identify all viable alternative actions and then fill in the *plus* and *minus* aspects for each. Some of you will cross off positive attributes that you see as being offset by equivalent negatives. Others will follow the oft-quoted Ben Franklin approach and cross off roughly-equal positives across alternatives, do the same for negatives, and then make a decision based on the factors "left standing." Some of you will just compare the number of positives and negatives across the board to gauge relative merit and some will attempt to refine the process—highlighting or emphasizing those aspects you deem more important than others.

The advantages of this approach are that it is simple to construct and is understood by everyone. The weaknesses are subtle but serious. Starting with the alternatives is equivalent to starting with the answers. This is a major mistake. Adding the plus and minus lists is, in reality, the process of "building a case" for and against each alternative—often with a bias or favorite in mind. Even if it is not your intent to build the case for your preferred choice, you will have created different decision criteria for each alternative—i. e., each alternative has its own unique list of positives and negatives. Each alternative is therefore held to a different standard.

Furthermore, whether or not you have "weighted" any elements, or crossed off any "equivalents", you may still have to explain or defend your conclusions. The lists of pluses and minuses are often expanded in these sessions and will usually set off a circular argument wherein each participant argues for the pluses in their favorite column and emphasizes the negatives in others. You know you are in a circular argument when you hear the words "yes, but" repeated around the table. This makes for very long meetings, wasted time, and frustrated participants. In the end, the decision will likely go to the most persuasive or powerful voice. If things do not go well, six months down the road everyone may have trouble explaining to *higher powers* just how this decision was made. "It seemed like a good idea at the time" will not do much for your career.

Is there a better way—a more sophisticated approach that is also fast, simple and usable by everyone? Is it possible to accelerate the collective decision process across a broad spectrum of different personalities? I am confident that the answer is *yes* but also that it will not be found in traditional decision theory.

Chapter III

THE NEED FOR A BETTER PROCESS

There is no status quo. Like it or not, nothing stays the same. Even in mature businesses, there are always changes and unexpected events. In younger businesses, these changes tend to be constant. Every manager knows he or she is operating in a *fluid environment* that keeps moving faster in a more aggressive world. Economic conditions, industry evolution, technological change, competitive actions, and internal effectiveness are always in some degree of flux. For most companies, the rates and magnitude of change have increased dramatically with the explosion of global competition, the acceleration of information flow, and the now-common geographic dispersion of operations.

All of these factors have put new pressures on corporate decision-making. This pressure applies not only to individuals but to entire organizations. Decisions must not only be better in a less-forgiving competitive environment, but also need to be made faster in step with a pace that, for the most part, will be driven by external forces.

Absence of a collaborative approach. Perhaps your organization has developed or adopted a consistent method for making decisions that is spread across the management structure. Perhaps it is effective enough to facilitate better decisions even when moving at high speed. If so, you belong to a rare company. In decades of exposure to entities large and small, smart to very smart, high-tech and otherwise, I have not found a management team with a common or efficient approach to decisions. It is unregulated territory and most managers have been left to find their own way; to develop their own personal approaches to decisions. Accordingly, most entities have inadvertently adopted an *ad hoc* collection of disparate approaches that will normally increase disagreement, slow the collective decision process, and narrow the sphere of influence over important decisions—i.e., the most persuasive or authoritative will eventually make the call—sometimes well and sometimes poorly but almost always after marathon meetings that consume an enormous amount of time and frustrate everyone.

Keeping the process simple and fast. To work at all levels of management and across the broad spectrum of everyday decisions, a successful process must meet this challenge. This is why sophisticated mathematical tools are rarely used by managers except as inputs from analysts. If the decision process is not easy to understand and communicate, it will not be used by many and will not be used often. This reality holds true for even the most complex decisions.

The process offered in this book is not about *theory* but about *reality*: the practical application of techniques shaped and tested by decades of use in a wide variety of businesses operating in difficult environments. It is based on a simple decision matrix that produces sophisticated answers. The process has been tested by exposure to thousands of issues and countless management teams of all stripes. It works. And, like many tools, the more you use it the better it will work for you. Any individual, who is willing to try, should find that it:

- is easy and quick to learn
- provides a consistent basis for better, faster decisions
- is applicable to any complex decision
- is applicable to all business functions and all levels of management
- easily combines sophisticated input with intuition and judgment
- provides a definitive record of why and how specific decisions were made

For management teams, there is broad potential to change the way decisions are made, communicated, revised, and recorded. For any group, it can:

- provide a vehicle to reach a consensus or sell a decision to other managers
- summarize results in ways that can be readily absorbed by upper management
- provide a vehicle to update or modify decisions rapidly to reflect new realities
- provide the basis for consistent decision-making across an entire culture.

Accomplishing these goals could produce a dramatic change in your own abilities to make better decisions and to make them faster. If embraced by an organization, the decision matrix could become a collaborative tool, a means of accelerating the management process, and a competitive weapon in a world where speed and better choices can materially impact results.

Chapter IV

RECOGNIZING A SIGNIFICANT DECISION

Most of the time it is obvious when there is a significant or important decision to make. Time, physical energy, and financial resources will be expended. Results will be expected and there will often be careful scrutiny of the outcome. However, sometimes it is not too obvious and yet the need for a good decision can be just as important. Here are four scenarios to make the point.

Few resources are required but serious consequences are possible. *A good example is driving a car too fast. It doesn't take much effort but many lives could be at stake around any bend in the road.* In a business sense, the same is true. It may not take much effort to change the price of a given product or service. Nevertheless, the consequences can be substantial. Increasing prices can result in higher profit margins or the loss of revenues and market share. Reducing prices can yield volume, cost, and market share benefits or diminish profitability and reduce return on investment. Just because there is no significant investment of resources doesn't mean it is not a serious decision.

An important decision needs to be made but you do not make it. This is a common mistake, especially in very busy or politically-charged environments. In these situations, it is likely that *time* will make the decision for you—i.e., if you procrastinate long enough, some good options will no longer be available. This does not mean you should make bad choices rather than no choices. It means that you should have a method to make consistent and rational choices faster—to become a more decisive manager without sacrificing the quality or your decisions.

Some decisions can be reversed and some cannot. This is one of the most important lessons in this book. Almost every decision you make will be impacted by the degree to which it is reversible. In personal life, it is easy to see the difference between choosing a hotel, buying a house, or having a baby. That pretty much covers the spectrum. In business, most important decisions are painful to reverse. In the pricing example above, if you were setting the price for several thousand retailers and it quickly became apparent that you overpriced the product, you might be able to offer discounts to "merchandise" your way out of the problem. If, however, you under-priced the product, you are probably stuck with the results—lost profits and inventory shortages until the next formal price-change opportunity, which could be months away.

A more serious example is the hiring of a key manager or executive. It is frequently a time-consuming and expensive process. Once you have made a choice, it is even more expensive to reverse the decision. This expense comes in two forms, obvious and hidden. The obvious aspects are the cost of a severance package and a repetition of the hiring process—i.e., management time, travel expenses, and perhaps heavy recruiting fees. The hidden aspects that are not so obvious, but often more expensive, are the loss of time and effectiveness for the directly-affected organization.

Let's assume you are hiring a new product manager for one of your most important product lines. He or she will have a major impact on new product directions and the effectiveness of the product team. While it might become apparent in six to twelve months that this manager is doing poorly on the product side, or the *people side* of the business, it is more likely that perceived success or failure will be tightly linked to the product development cycle—i.e., when the new products for which this manager is responsible start hitting the market. If the development cycle is generally two years in length, it would probably be two or three years before it can be determined that this product manager has failed and should be replaced.

In this example, the years are lost. They are years in which your competitors may have made better product decisions and now have a stronger market position and a platform to broaden a lead over you. There is no way to counter this consequence. In addition, your new product manager faces a challenge bigger than his or her predecessor—to *leapfrog* the competition and regain lost market share and momentum. And, he or she must do this while learning a new business, working with a new group, and developing a good working relationship with many other functions. A second hiring mistake would probably be fatal to the business in this example.

In general, the higher the position, the more resources are affected. Reversing one to several years of bad decisions can be extremely expensive or impossible. For some very large examples, think about the plethora of high-profile mergers and acquisitions that have gone awry with devastating results. Think about how hard it has been for these companies to reverse the consequences.

Be certain that every decision criterion incorporates a consideration of *reversibility* in some appropriate from. In business, *it is hard to rewind the clock.*

Some decisions are preemptive. It is important to recognize when a decision is going to have a *preemptive effect* on other possible choices. If a decision is going to limit your business options down the road you are, *de facto*, making two or more decisions at one time—i.e., the direction you have chosen and any or all of the others that will no longer be available to you.

For example, if you are about to sign a five-year agreement with a national network of independent sales representatives, you should recognize that you are preempting your ability to exercise tighter control over the sales process with an in-house team. If you enter into a strategic partnership with one business partner, you may be preempting a potential relationship with every other similar entity.

On the other hand, if you are signing an agreement with a vendor for a specific product or service, it should not preclude you from also buying products and services from other vendors.

The magic word is *exclusivity*. Any terms of agreement that include the words *exclusive rights* or *exclusivity* should send up red flares around the conference table. These are clear signals that you are about to enter into a preemptive agreement. If possible, negotiate the elimination of any such terms. If exclusivity is a necessary aspect of a critical agreement, find a way to put limits on it. These can be quantitative performance requirements, time limits, geographical limits, specific exceptions to the rule, reasonable terms for dissolution of the contract, or a mixture of all of the above.

Be careful with preemptive decisions. *When opportunity knocks, you should have your hands free to open the door.*

Chapter V

BUILDING A DECISION MATRIX

The key to better decisions. A decision matrix is a simple but powerful way to *frame* any important decision. It provides a mechanism to combine all considerations—both quantitative and qualitative. The end product is an optimal view of all relevant factors displayed in the context of what you want to achieve. When applied to standard benchmarks, it will generate confidence, consistency, and better business results. The purpose of this book is to make you an expert in the effective use of this tool.

Starting with objectives. Many of the strategic planners I have worked with were fond of saying *"If you don't know where you are going, any road will get you there."* This same warning has been stated by many people in many different ways—but the message is consistent: if you don't have a good set of goals or objectives, then your application of time, energy, and money will probably take you somewhere else. For example, there are several major highways leading out of Chicago. You are currently driving on one. Is it the best road for you? I think you get the idea.

It is important that semantics not get in the way of your thought process regarding goals and objectives. For some people, these terms suggest a formality that is often not productive. Learn to think in broader terms about positive results—they many come in many forms.

- Formal and informal business goals
- Positive attributes of any business scenario
- Positive consequences of any considered action
- Any results that would be favorable to your business
- Short term and long term advantages

For the sake of brevity going forward, I will refer to any desirable result as a "goal." Think of these goals in the broadest possible sense and do not, under any circumstances, limit them to official or formal corporate objectives. These are the elements you will want to maximize in a positive sense. Avoidance of negative consequences should normally be addressed independently with other downside potential or "risks" (addressed later in this chapter).

A comprehensive list of goals will become the foundation of every matrix and will be critical to superior results. Once you get used to starting this way consistently, the decision process should become faster and easier—it should become *second nature* to you.

Case number one—compensation structure. *A large insurance company was considering a fundamental change in the way all employees were compensated. The CFO had recommended that the traditional practice of annual pay raises be replaced by a pay-for-performance approach for all salaried employees. He argued that, even with modest increases of 3% to 5% per year, overall compensation was compounding at a rate in excess of industry standards and inflation benchmarks. He also argued that poorer performing employees were receiving annual increases roughly equivalent to those of better performing employees—an inequity that was affecting morale.*

In essence, he was suggesting that the entire compensation system be structured more like the one used for executives where bonuses tied to performance were favored over salary increases. The CEO was favorably inclined but others around the conference table were not so sure. Division heads were somewhat interested but had some concerns about how it would be implemented. The human resources manager thought it might turn into an administrative nightmare for HR and might demoralize many employees while increasing the burden on functional managers up and down the line. Nevertheless, it was hard to argue with the basic concept of containing overall compensation expenses while rewarding the most productive employees.

One compromise was suggested wherein executives would get their normal bonuses but each division would get a "team bonus" based on performance in lieu of individual bonuses.

The group decided to meet again on the topic after a comprehensive list of advantages and disadvantages had been constructed by the CFO with inputs from all participants. The resulting summary follows.

<u>Alternative A – the status quo</u>. Executives continue to receive bonuses of 25% to 50%, mid-level managers would receive bonuses from 10% to 25%, and the balance of salaried employees would get their standard raise of 3% to 5%.

Perceived positives

+   *Compensation system understood by all employees.*
+   *No additional burden on managers at any level.*
+   *No risk of demoralizing employees not receiving bonuses.*
+   *Risks of a major change avoided.*
+   *No new burden on the Human Resources organization.*

Perceived negatives

-    *Annual costs of compensation keep rising*
-    *Many overachievers do not get rewarded*
-    *Some key personnel are not motivated*

Alternative B – pay for personal performance. All salaried employees would be eligible for a bonus. These payouts would be based on performance against specific corporate, functional, and personal goals. Bonuses would range from 5% to 50% but, in total, would be capped to ensure an annual savings in overall compensation expense. Each manager would be responsible for tracking performance and recommending bonuses for his or her own team. Pay increases would be allowed but would largely be replaced by the pay-for-performance incentive.

Perceived positives

+   *Cost containment.*
+   *Minimize fixed expense—protection for a soft year.*
+   *Maximum incentives for all employees.*
+   *Management leverage at all levels.*
+   *Retention of key employees.*
+   *High morale for overachievers.*
+   *Maximum system fairness.*
+   *Better corporate results.*

<u>*Perceived negatives*</u>

- *Management effort needed to establish goals and track performance.*
- *Heightened concerns about bonus favoritism.*
- *Demoralization for those receiving smallest or no bonuses.*
- *Complication of the system—employee confusion.*
- *Additional burden on human resources function.*
- *Difficult to return to traditional system if it fails.*

<u>*Alternative C – hybrid: bonus pay for divisional performance*</u>. *All executives and high-level managers would continue to receive individual bonuses but lower level managers and all salaried employees would share in a "team bonus" based on their division's performance against specific goals.*

<u>*Perceived positives*</u>

- *Standard incentives in place for high level managers.*
- *Increased incentives for better teamwork within each division.*
- *More emphasis on corporate results.*
- *Some containment of fixed compensation expense.*
- *Minimal impact on management process and HR requirements.*
- *Fairly easy transition back to traditional system if necessary.*

<u>*Perceived negatives*</u>

- *Employee concerns that one division will be favored over another.*
- *Overachievers below middle management receive same bonus as the less productive.*
- *Difficulties in establishing performance goals for different businesses.*
- *Limited management ability to motivate individual employees.*

This looked like a difficult decision. Compensation is typically the largest line item for most businesses and goes to the heart of the organization's ability to function—its people. On one hand, it is what keeps a business going and, on the other, can drive down profits, make the company less competitive, and make it harder to pay for other rising costs such as healthcare. Given the lists above, it should be no surprise that the management team debated the alternatives at great length.

The more aggressive members of the staff favored pay for performance strongly as a way to contain costs, reward key contributors, motivate all employees, and empower managers at all levels. The more conservative members were nervous about such a substantial change in structure. They were not convinced of the wisdom of either of the other two choices and argued for the status quo. Some division managers were adamant that the "hybrid" approach would give them a much-needed tool to increase productivity and morale in their own operations. At the same time, they were apprehensive about what their assigned goals might be. In the end, there was no clear answer and the issue was tabled for discussion at a future date.

If "tabled" long enough, time and indecision will favor the *status quo*—the most common answer for difficult decisions. As is the case with most business issues, the strengths of one alternative will be the weaknesses of another. The debate can go back and forth endlessly as each alternative is brought up by a supporting party and then undermined by opponents. If you are making a decision on your own, you may still bounce from one alternative to another trapped by the opposing strengths and weaknesses of each choice. This is the "decision trap" that often produces inaction, or less than optimal actions.

A decision matrix is a completely different way to frame an issue. It is simple to construct and will change the way every decision looks. In most cases, what was unclear becomes obvious. Follow the next seven steps to see how it works. With a small amount of practice, you should become proficient at producing consistently-good results. The process begins by backing away from alternatives and looking at objectives first.

Step one—making a list of goals. This list should be expansive to ensure that no important goals or advantages are ignored. From the case material above, we might construct the set shown below. I have grouped them for purposes of clarity. Those that were stated in the case material as objectives but are more appropriately categorized as downside risks (e.g. potential employee confusion) are listed in similar fashion on a subsequent list. These are the positives:

Company performance
   + *Maximize employee productivity*
   + *Minimize fixed expenses to protect profit in soft years*
   + *Contain the spiraling costs of compensation*
   + *Expand profits or funds available for other programs*

Employee motivation
+ *Provide incentives for all employees*
+ *Reward overachievers for actual performance*
+ *Retain key contributors*
+ *Encourage more teamwork at all levels*
+ *Maximize employee morale*

Management process
+ *Enhance management leverage and control—ability to reward selectively*
+ *Enhance management ability to motivate all salaried employees*
+ *Facilitate the overall management process*

Human Resources
+ *Keep the compensation system simple*
+ *Facilitate the HR process*

Step two—eliminating duplications and similar items. This is very important. Duplication will distort results by inadvertently overemphasizing one category and thereby diluting others. It is critical in Step one to *cast a wider net*. Now, it is necessary to condense the list in order to avoid the dilution of double counting—i.e., listing a goal twice by virtue of different wording (see Chapter VI for more discussion). Note that goals do not need to be listed in any particular order. Also expect that some of them will be conflicting—this will almost always be the case. Do not try to resolve conflicts at this point as sorting them out will be the primary role of the matrix. In our example, Step two reduces the number of goals from fourteen to seven.

+ *Increase corporate productivity—motivate all employees*
+ *Reward actual performance—retain key employees*
+ *Enhance management leverage*
+ *Contain compensation expense—minimize fixed expense*
+ *Keep compensation system simple—avoid employee confusion*
+ *Encourage corporate teamwork at all levels*
+ *Facilitate the HR process*

Step three—determining the most important goal. This is a critical step and will play a key role in the validity of end results. It is based entirely on the assignment of the number TEN. Ten is the highest value you can assign to any goal. Here are the simple rules for its application.

- Ten is always the starting point for assigning values or weights to all goals and objectives.
- You must assign a 10 to the most important goal on the list—always do this first.
- You can only use the number 10 once. It is necessary to force this distinction.
- Review the list carefully and assign a 10 to the most important goal.

As you will see below, I have rated "Contain compensation expense" as the most important goal and assigned it a value of ten (note: the labels are abbreviated for simplicity and space).

Weighting the most important goal

GOALS	RELATIVE IMPORTANCE
Increase corporate productivity	
Reward actual performance	
Enhance management leverage	
Contain compensation expense	**10**
Minimize system complexity	
Encourage corporate teamwork	
Facilitate the HR process	

Step four—determining the relative importance or "weight" of each goal. Rate each goal independently versus the one deemed most important; this is your standard for comparison. Follow the rules below.

- Do not change the random order of the list (it may introduce bias).
- Start at the top and rate each goal's importance relative to the one that received the ten. Compare each to the most important rather than to each other.
- Use numbers one to nine only.

- Use 1-9 as many times as you see fit. You do not need to use them all. This is not a traditional forced ranking.
- When you have finished, compare the weightings of each one against all others to check for balance—to see if you have over- or understated the importance of any item. Refine the weightings accordingly.

It is important to differentiate. Do not overvalue every goal on the list. For example, something that is almost as important as your most important item might receive an 8 or 9. Something of much lesser importance might be assigned a 1, 2, or perhaps a 3. You don't have to be perfect—the technique is designed to work with approximations. You are quantifying judgments and that can only be done with estimates. For this example, I completed Step four with the following result.

Weighting all goals

GOALS	WEIGHT
Increase corporate productivity	9
Reward actual performance	7
Enhance management leverage	5
Contain compensation expense	**10**
Minimize system complexity	4
Encourage corporate teamwork	6
Facilitate the HR process	3

This is for example purposes only. If this decision were being debated in your company, you might have a different set of objectives and would have weightings that reflect your own company priorities. Nevertheless, the process would be exactly the same. Having determined the goals and their relative values, the process can accelerate now with limited effort.

Step five—determining the relative strength of each alternative. This is where we begin to make rapid progress. In this step, we can add the number zero to the range of possible scores. It should be used judiciously but in some cases is a better reflection of reality. Note: zero should never be used as a "goal weight" as a goal of no importance should be excluded from consideration for obvious reasons. Now use the new range of zero to ten horizontally—across the matrix line by line. This intrinsically supports a higher level of objectivity while undermining any conscious (or subconscious) effort to "engineer" or force a desired outcome. The next section should make this clear.

- Go to the first goal in the matrix. Ignore all others. You must address one line at a time. Look across the alternatives and assign a 10 to the one that best "fits" that goal. Assigning the ten does not mean it is a perfect fit but only that it is a better fit than any of the other choices.

- Recognize that all decisions are combinations of the known and the unknown. Do your best to assess relative merit. You are looking into the future—you may be able establish mathematical probabilities for some events but most will be based on best judgments. This is greatly facilitated by the fact that you are assigning relative merit and not absolute merit—i.e., the best of the group rather than the ability to accomplish the goal. Chapter IX will offer a test for absolute merit.

- The more precise you can be, the better the result. Regardless, the process employs a weighted average across several dimensions and will consistently produce good results even with a mixture of subjective estimates. Do your homework where necessary to refine scoring and then move ahead.

- Completely ignore the importance weighting* you have given each goal. Focus only on the relative merit of each alternative and disregard their assigned importance. This will add to the validity of end results. My scoring for the first line item (row) might look like this:

Scoring the first goal

GOALS	WT	Status quo: Annual raise	Pay for performance	Division bonus
Corporate productivity	*	1	10	7

Assessment—the pay-for-performance alternative receives the highest score because it would provide motivation for all salaried employees to work harder. The hybrid scores well because, while not providing an individual incentive to all, it would still motivate top management with their normal bonus package and would also motivate all salaried personnel in each division to work harder for higher pay. The traditional approach of small annual raises for the vast majority of employees would provide very little motivation and certainly no new incentives for greater effort. Continue the process as follows.

- After scoring the first, go on to the second and so on until you have finished with scores for every goal.

- Don't let the scoring of any single line influence the scoring for any other. Each line should represent an independent consideration.

- As before, you must use ten once (and once only) in each row but you can use any numbers from 0-9 as many times as you wish. Try to differentiate as carefully as possible. Resist the temptation to give each alternative a high score. There is a simple way to test for over- weighting that will be discussed later. Here's what the matrix would look like with the rest of my scoring:

Scoring all goals

GOALS	WT	Status quo: Annual raise	Pay for performance	Division bonus
Corporate productivity	9	1	10	7
Reward actual performance	7	2	10	7
Enhance management leverage	5	2	10	7
Contain compensation expense	10	3	10	8
Minimize system complexity	4	10	3	7
Encourage corporate teamwork	6	1	3	10
Facilitate the HR process	3	10	2	7

Assessment—the pay-for-performance option clearly offers the most managerial leverage, expense control, and employee motivation. However, the division bonus would also motivate people to work harder, would encourage team effort in a way that individual bonuses might undermine, and is much easier to administer—i.e., division goals are much easier to establish and track than individual goals. The simplest approach is the traditional approach but it has little to offer in terms of motivation or management control.

Key process note—it should be clear that we have **separated the relative importance of each goal from the ability of each alternative to accomplish it**. This distinction is critical to the value of the matrix and also the ability to escape the *circular box* of conflicting advantages and disadvantages.

We are now in position to generate our first solid answer. We have a refined set of carefully weighted goals and we have determined how well or poorly each considered alternative fits the criteria on a "relative basis."

Step six—determining a weighted fit. The next step is straightforward and always interesting. Simply multiply the value of each goal by the score each alternative received, line-by-line. Adding them up will give us a new perspective on how well each alternative fits the weighted criteria. Very frequently, these totals will reveal surprising differences that were not apparent when advantages and disadvantages were compared without benefit of the matrix.

Calculating a weighted fit

Alternatives →		Status quo: Annual raise		Pay for performance		Division bonus	
GOALS	WT	SCORE	PTS	SCORE	PTS	SCORE	PTS
Increase corporate productivity	9	1	9	10	90	7	63
Reward actual performance	7	2	14	10	70	7	49
Enhance management leverage	5	2	10	10	50	7	35
Contain compensation expense	10	3	30	10	100	8	80
Minimize system complexity	4	10	40	3	12	7	28
Encourage corporate teamwork	6	1	6	3	18	10	60
Facilitate the HR process	3	10	30	2	6	7	21
TOTAL POINTS		139		346		336	

Observation—total points are representations of the overall weighted fit—how well each alternative measures up against the decision criteria. They are abstract numbers and are not meaningful in an absolute sense. However, they are very definitive in terms of how well or poorly each alternative fares against every other alternative. In order to make answers easier to understand and more useful, it is often worthwhile to convert these sums to percentages. This is done by comparing each total score to the total number of points possible—that is, a perfect score. The basis for this is the total of all weights x 10. This could only happen if one alternative had received a 10 for every objective. A simple calculation produces the following:

Converting to % of maximum possible score

Alternatives →	WT	Status quo: Annual raise		Pay for performance		Hybrid: Division bonus	
GOALS	WT	SCORE	PTS	SCORE	PTS	SCORE	PTS
Increase corporate productivity	9	1	9	10	90	7	63
Reward actual performance	7	2	14	10	70	7	49
Enhance management leverage	5	2	10	10	50	7	35
Contain compensation expense	10	3	30	10	100	8	80
Minimize system complexity	4	10	40	3	12	7	28
Encourage corporate teamwork	6	1	6	3	18	10	60
Facilitate the HR process	3	10	30	2	6	7	21
TOTAL (ALL WEIGHTS)	44						
MAXIMUM POSSIBLE POINTS	440	139		346		336	
% OF MAXIMUM POINTS	100%	32%		79%		76%	

Conclusion—it is clear that the status quo offers little in the context of company objectives. It is also clear that both of the more "leveraged" plans offer a high degree of fit with weighted objectives but for different reasons. This is a very positive picture in that it provides a clear understanding of specific strengths and weakness for each alternative. It also demonstrates clearly why traditional decision approaches can create conflict and endless debate.

In order to complete the decision process, the approach applied to "goals" must now be applied to "risks"—the potential negative consequences for each alternative. As this is a very important decision with broad impact on company operations, the risks are significant. The following is a condensed list of six drawn from the case material.

Compensation decision risks

- *Inequities in performance measures. It may be reasonably easy to establish performance goals for a division but very difficult to establish goals by individual. Quantitative goals may be hard to establish for many positions and qualitative benchmarks (such as teamwork, reliability, effort, knowledge, skill development, etc.) will be even tougher and more arbitrary.*

- *Uneven management application. This is a concern that individual managers, even with the best of intentions, may not be able to develop and apply consistent performance measures across the broad spectrum of functions and individuals. Some will be more generous than others and it will be difficult for senior managers or HR to sort out the disparities.*

- *Loss of key people. This is a concern that a significant number of overachievers including those with long term high potential may leave the Company. While higher level managers can be motivated and retained with individual bonuses, many younger employees, at lower levels, may be trapped in a layered salary structure that offers little in terms of near-term rewards.*

- *Negative impact on morale. This looks like a duplication but is a different risk. This is a general concern about the impact of making a substantial change in the compensation system and the potential confusion that might go along with it. It would be near zero for the status quo and very high for the individual bonus plan. The division plan would discourage some but encourage others. A good plan should balance these two aspects and minimize the level of risk for morale deterioration.*

- *Potential for management abuse. This is the risk that employees will perceive that managers are intentionally "playing favorites" in both the establishment of performance goals and also the assessment of accomplishment. It may well be an instinctive error but it is also a very real possibility. It is a high risk for the pay-for-performance plan but a low risk for the others.*

- *Difficult to return to the status quo. This is the reversibility issue discussed in Chapter IV. The status quo should receive a rare "zero" for this risk as there is no departure from current practices. Moving to a pay-for-performance system wherein higher achievers receive extra compensation would be very hard to reverse. The very people you wanted to reward and retain, would now be penalized the most by reverting to the standard annual raise approach. The division bonus plan would have a much easier path back to the traditional approach as the key individual impact would be greatly lessened.*

Step seven—determining relative risk. The exact same approach is used for risks with one exception—the use of "zero to 10" is reversed for scoring alternatives. Zero is used to indicate no risk at all and ten to indicate greatest comparative risk. The higher the total score, the higher the level of risk. Evaluating risk is addressed separately to reflect the fact that risks and negatives are distinct from goals, are derived from different considerations, and are not technically offset by positive aspects—i.e., they will always be present. This separate treatment also serves to avoid the *blurring* of a decision that occurs when risks and negatives are lumped together with objectives, goals, and advantages.

Even if our abilities to see into the future are limited, it is not hard to approximate the likelihood of disappointing results. Here are some guidelines for best results:

- The list of possible risks should be generated in the same random fashion as the list of goals. This helps to keep bias out of the scoring.

- There will be an initial tendency to create a list that looks like the flip side of goals—e.g., if a key objective is to reach $100 million in revenues, then you may instinctively want to include a risk such as "failure to reach revenue targets." This form of duplication should not be applied broadly but can be appropriate on a selective basis.

  For example, one strategy that could maximize revenues might be conventional and less risky while another with the same potential might be outside the box and inherently more risky. In this case, comparing the risk levels will serve to differentiate alternatives and therefore be helpful. A small amount of experience will help you minimize overlap. One simple rule: if a stated goal looks like the "avoidance" of a negative result, move it to the risk section. In addition, make sure that all real risks are addressed—leaving out just one significant risk could produce faulty decisions.

- Do not include any risks that are identical for all alternatives. Recognize, however, that this is rarely the case. Even a difference in scoring of 10 versus 9 or 8 could be important and therefore should be included. Review seemingly identical scores carefully. If they are truly the same for all alternatives, leave them out.

- Make sure all risk criteria consider how hard it would be to alter or reverse course if reality diverges from expectations. This is the reversibility factor, and should never be left out of any decision.

For this example, I assigned the highest weight to those risks that make the new system difficult to execute, have the greatest potential impact on employees, and make retreating to a traditional approach difficult. The subsequent scoring of alternatives produced dramatic results.

Summary of risks by alternative

Alternatives →		Status quo: Annual raise		Pay for performance		Hybrid: division bonus	
RISKS	WT	SCORE	PTS	SCORE	PTS	SCORE	PTS
Performance measure inequities	10	2	*20*	10	*100*	5	*50*
Uneven management application	7	3	*21*	10	*70*	4	*28*
Negative impact on morale	6	7	*42*	10	*60*	3	*18*
Potential management abuse	5	2	*10*	10	*50*	3	*15*
Loss of key people	8	10	*80*	3	*24*	5	*40*
Difficult to return to *status quo*	6	0	*0*	10	*60*	4	*24*
TOTAL (ALL WEIGHTS)	42						
MAXIMUM POSSIBLE POINTS	420	*173*		*364*		*175*	
% OF MAXIMUM POINTS	*100%*	*41%*		*87%*		*42%*	

Key process note—these numbers are not mathematically comparable to the numerical totals for goals. They are based on different criteria with different weights. If goals and objectives are *apples*, these are *oranges*. They may end up in the same basket but they are different. They must be judged independently.

The conversion to *percentage of maximum fit* does not make them comparable either, but does allow for an overall perspective—the degree to which a given alternative satisfies comprehensive goals and, at the same time, the degree to which it avoids risk. Often this perspective is enhanced by comparing results graphically. In essence, one graph can combine every assumption, every value, and the relative merits of every viable alternative into a single picture.

Total weighted fit for goals and risks

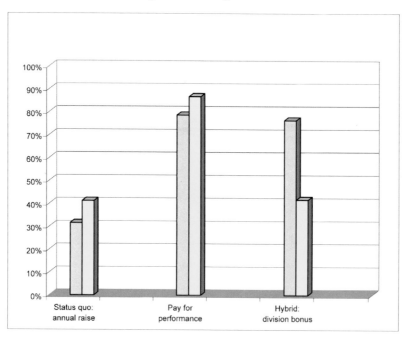

Conclusion—while two alternatives display comparable advantages measured against weighted goals (grey), a very different picture emerges when risks (yellow) are considered. The pay-for-performance concept has an extremely high level of risk both in terms of implementation and correction if flawed. The concept of a new "division bonus program" demonstrates a comparable level of advantages but has dramatically lower risk. For all of its advantages, it has little more risk than doing nothing—i.e., staying with the status quo. It would also be a fine interim step. If it works well, it can be fine-tuned judiciously to make the Company more productive while controlling costs. If results are disappointing, it can largely

be reversed by moving the division incentives back towards more traditional annual pay raises. What initially appeared to be a difficult decision now looks clear-cut.

The above example is not unusual. Alternatives that are roughly equal in terms of meeting goals and objectives often look different in terms of risk. Always consider potential negative consequences independently and carefully. They frequently make the difference. Note: this consideration is not intended to make managers pessimistic or indecisive—quite the opposite. A careful assessment of both sides of the equation in this manner will clearly identify the most important advantages to press and the most significant risks to avoid. In the end, management should be more decisive and empowered to make bolder choices.

Postscript: the actual insurance company used to build this example did, in the end, decide to implement the "pay-for-performance" bonus program for all salaried employees. As you can see from the exhibits in this chapter, I would not have made the same choice.

Chapter VI

CRITERIA COMPRESSION

The case for compression. In Chapter V, the lists of goals and risks were initially expanded and thereafter compressed. This step is so important that it bears repeating and further example. There are two different dynamics at work. The first is expanding the initial lists to make sure that nothing important is left out. You do not want to finalize your decision, and perhaps communicate it to others in the Company, only to find out that you have failed to consider an important goal or significant risk. It is important to be thorough.

The second step is condensing or compressing both lists (goals and risks) in order to avoid duplication and facilitate better scoring—any duplication can overstate the importance of several smaller considerations while understating the value of your most important factors. It is simple math—the pie can only have so many pieces before there are no big ones left. Case number two dramatizes the value of compression.

Case number two—choosing a strategic partner. *A young software company had reached a business impasse at the $10 million dollar revenue level. They had exhausted all internal resources to reach this point. The sales force was completely overextended. It was facing increased competition, longer sales cycles, and manpower limitations. The technical support group could no longer keep up with incoming requests and complaints and began relying on the software development team to provide adequate customer support. This demoralized the development team and caused postponement of critical product improvements and new product initiatives. Even though this was a leading edge enterprise, competitors were beginning to outpace the Company and a much larger marketing effort was needed to maintain a high-profile industry presence. To make matters worse, the Company was facing a financial crisis and needed new investment.*

The management team felt the only way out of this predicament was to gain the support of a strategic partner—preferably a large "player" that could provide the "business muscle" necessary to survive and compete. Because the Company held a conceptual leadership position in a rapid-growth industry *segment, many large companies had expressed interest in a business relationship. The candidate companies ranged in size from $50 million to over $500 million in revenues and were all strong enough to be viable partners. Choosing the best partner was the challenge—all of the candidates brought something different to the equation and the Company only had the energy to support one partnership at this time. They also needed to make the decision quickly.*

Two companies stood out as the strongest potential partners—the first brought marketing savvy and power while the second offered investment and financial strength. This set up a classic decision dilemma wherein each alternative exhibited different strengths and weaknesses and the debate began moving in circles. In this case, the software company needed the advantages of both but could only pick one. The following are thumbnail sketches of the two partnership candidates.

Major Marketing Company—this company had strong brand recognition, a very competitive sales operation, and strong public relations capabilities. Their technology platform was compatible and the potential for joint marketing was strong. They had a relaxed style that boded well for future management "chemistry" but were inclined towards exclusivity—an inclination that might contractually preempt other opportunities in the years ahead.

Major Financial Company—this was a very large company that was primarily interested in becoming an investor while using the Company's software for internal operations. As such, they might become a marquee reference account but had no marketing expertise or resources. Their management team would be less involved; meaning less potential influence or distraction but also less support. Their contractual style was more demanding but they had little interest in tying the Company's hands in terms of other partnerships. They would protect their investment but would not preempt opportunities outside the financial segment.

As this was a matter of survival, the Company's management team needed to make the best possible decision: there would only be one chance. As a group, they made a weighted list of all goals and risks.

Strategic partner criteria

Goals	*Weight*
Good executive "chemistry"	*8*
Supportive management team	*6*
Compatible corporate cultures	*6*
Reasonable contract terms	*5*
Long term merger potential	*3*
Financial support (investment)	*9*
Revenue growth enhancement	*10*
Minimal management effort	*9*
Enhanced profitability	*6*
Sales process support	*5*
Balanced joint effort	*6*
Public relations capability	*6*
Strengthened industry presence	*7*
Competitive leverage	*8*
Expanded market exposure	*2*
Total—all weights	*96*

Risks	*Weight*
Management distraction	*10*
Drain on development resources	*7*
Complication of sales process	*8*
Preemption of other opportunities	*7*
Duplication of effort	*2*
Failure to execute or sustain effort	*7*
Lack of ongoing investment	*4*
Difficult to terminate relationship	*8*
Total—all weights	*53*

Key process note—while it might have been possible to generate a valid decision matrix at this point, it would have been awkward and sub-optimal.

- There were too many goals to differentiate effectively.
- There were many goals that were borderline duplications (e.g. executive chemistry and supportive management or industry presence and public relations).
- The most important factors (revenue growth and investment) were overshadowed by combinations of items of lesser importance that were not critical to survival.

In order to optimize results, both lists were compressed with the following result.

Strategic partner—Compressed criteria

GOALS	WEIGHT	NOTES
Positive corporate chemistry	7	Executive chemistry, support, compatibility.
Financial support	9	Initial investment with additional potential.
Revenue growth enhancement	10	Sales, revenue, and profit support.
Minimal management effort	8	Minimal management/resources required.
Competitive & industry leverage	7	PR, market presence, competitive advantage.
Long term merger potential	3	Natural synergy, balanced effort, contract terms.
TOTAL	**44**	

RISKS	WEIGHT	NOTES
Management distraction	10	Largest risk due to fragile position.
Internal resource stress	9	Development, support, and sales at limits.
Preemption of other opportunity	7	Down the road but could be critical.
Failure to sustain effort	7	Partner's priorities change after initial effort.
Difficult to terminate agreement	8	Critical risk if partnership not working.
TOTAL	**41**	

At this point, with a tighter set of criteria, it was relatively easy to compare and score the two alternatives.

Strategic partner—Decision matrix

Alternatives →		Major Marketing Company		Major Financial Company	
GOALS	WEIGHT	SCORE	PTS	SCORE	PTS
Positive corporate "chemistry"	7	10	*70*	4	*28*
Financial support	9	1	*9*	10	*90*
Revenue growth enhancement	10	10	*100*	2	*20*
Minimal management effort	8	4	*32*	10	*80*
Competitive & industry leverage	7	10	*70*	3	*21*
Long term merger potential	3	10	*30*	3	*9*
TOTAL (ALL WEIGHTS)	44	*311*		*248*	
MAXIMUM POSSIBLE POINTS	*440*				
% OF MAXIMUM POINTS	*100%*	**71%**		**56%**	

RISKS	WEIGHT	SCORE	PTS	SCORE	PTS
Management distraction	10	10	*100*	2	*20*
Internal resource stress	9	10	*90*	1	*9*
Preemption of other opportunity	7	10	*70*	2	*14*
Failure to sustain effort	7	4	*28*	10	*70*
Difficult to terminate agreement	8	10	*80*	2	*16*
TOTAL (ALL WEIGHTS)	41	*368*		*129*	
MAXIMUM POSSIBLE POINTS	*410*				
% OF MAXIMUM POINTS	*100%*	**90%**		**31%**	

Conclusion—the management team was not happy with these results. Clearly there were important benefits with Major Marketing in terms of chemistry, market leverage, revenue growth and long term considerations. However, these advantages came with much higher risks of distracting the Company, ty-

ing up resources, preempting other opportunities, and enforcing contract terms. Unable to think of ways to diminish these risks, management decided to approach Major Financial to see if there were ways to strengthen the positive aspects of a potential relationship. From one high-level meeting, they received a commitment from Major Financial to not only invest in the Company and to broadly use its products internally, but also to serve as a marketing partner. In this role, they would provide a powerful reference for new prospects, entertain site visits, publicize use of the Company's products to the press, and participate in trade show events They had become more enthusiastic about the strategic value of the partnership and saw the expansion of their role as a way to increase their return on investment.

When these changes were reflected in the decision matrix (increasing the relative fit for revenue growth enhancement and industry leverage), a different picture emerged.

Goals criteria—Revised fit

Alternatives →		Major Marketing Company		Major Financial Company	
GOALS	WEIGHT	SCORE	PTS	SCORE	PTS
Positive corporate "chemistry"	7	10	70	4	28
Financial support	9	1	9	10	90
Revenue growth enhancement	10	10	100	⑤	50
Minimal management effort	8	4	32	10	80
Competitive & industry leverage	7	10	70	⑦	49
Long term merger potential	3	10	30	3	9
TOTAL (ALL WEIGHTS)	44	311		306	
MAXIMUM POSSIBLE POINTS	440				
% OF MAXIMUM POINTS	100%	71%		70%	

While the risk profiles were unchanged, the prospects for goals achievement were now essentially equal. With the dramatic differences in risk level, the decision became clear. Once again the summary graphic provided a good overall perspective.

Total weighted fit for goals and risks

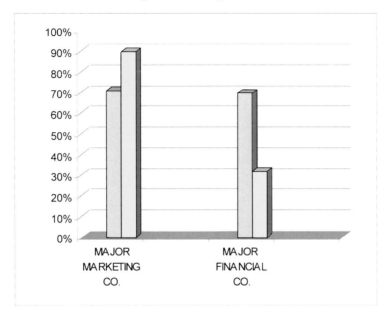

Key process note—if the matrix fails to produce a decisive result, there are three options.

1. Go back and re-examine all assumptions. Do not try to force results but to look for valid refinements. In this case, there were no **realistic refinements** that would change the outcome.
2. Look for **better alternatives**. In this case, the Company needed to move quickly to survive and these were the best options available in the near term.
3. Look for ways to **modify alternatives** in order to make them a better fit with business requirements. In this case, expanding the marketing role of one option created a higher level of fit with goals at a relatively low level of risk.

In option one, it is important not to get *creative*. You do not want to distort assessments in order to make the results look better when, in fact, it will result in a poor decision. For options two and three, the challenge is the opposite—to be creative in order to materially improve an alternative or to seek new alternatives. This last dictum is often critical to success and is the topic of the next chapter.

Chapter VII

CREATIVE ALTERNATIVES

There is always a better way. Perhaps the primary reason that many business decisions are ill-conceived, or less-than-optimal, is because the best alternative is never considered. Just as it is important to be expansive in criteria development, so also is it critical in the determination of viable alternatives. While many executives are not comfortable with new ideas, they are often vastly superior to conventional choices. Creative alternatives usually come from three sources:

1. A combination of two or more conventional options.
2. A new idea that fits within traditional boundaries.
3. A completely new idea from "outside the box."

The following case not only demonstrates the potential value of adding a creative alternative but also the power of the matrix to sell that alternative to upper management. There is no better internal sales tool than the quantification of benefits versus a logical set of business goals (see Chapter XI).

Case number three—a capacity and marketing dilemma. *A large manufacturer of consumer products was gaining ground on foreign competition when a key manufacturing location reported a problem—the latest sales projections would exceed annual capacity by approximately 20%. Strained to the limit, this plant was struggling with quality issues while trying to deal with the poorest productivity numbers in the Company. It was an old facility and was scheduled for shutdown and replacement within three years.*

In the meantime, the affected marketing group would have to make some difficult choices. It was under widespread corporate pressure from upper management to raise prices to reflect general inflationary pressures and the issue of capacity limits would surely make this pressure more severe.

At the same time, there was a unique opportunity to boost sales and market share as the sales force was well on its way to achieving record orders for the year. Torn between the opposing forces of politics, capacity, quality, and market opportunity, the marketing team had few choices. Basically it could:

1. *Hold the current course—try to convince upper management that raising prices would injure a strong competitive posture, explain to the sales force that there was no escape from capacity limitations (putting limits on sales commissions), and accept the loss of market opportunity.*

2. *Implement price increases—accommodate upper management pressure, increase profit margins, improve return on investment, maintain quality, and accept the loss of market share from both higher prices and limited capacity.*

3. *Outsource production—contract with a qualified vendor (Far East) to produce the high-demand core products under "private label." This would not be popular with some in top management but would support higher sales and market share. The morale of the sales force would be restored but delivery timing, quality control, and shorter margins would all be critical issues.*

The decision matrix made the "pull" of opposing forces obvious and frustrating.

Capacity and marketing dilemma—Decision matrix I

Alternatives →		Hold current course		Increase prices		Outsource production	
GOALS	WEIGHT	SCORE	PTS	SCORE	PTS	SCORE	PTS
Maximize profit margins	10	7	70	10	100	5	50
Maximize ROI	8	7	56	10	80	5	40
Maximize sales & mkt share	9	7	63	4	36	10	90
Maintain field sales morale	6	6	36	3	18	10	60
Maintain customer loyalty	7	7	49	3	21	10	70
Optimize plant utilization	5	9	45	10	50	5	25
TOTAL (ALL WEIGHTS)	45	319		305		335	
MAX. POSSIBLE POINTS	450						
% OF MAXIMUM POINTS	100%	71%		68%		74%	

Capacity and marketing dilemma—Decision matrix I (cont'd)

Alternatives →		Hold current course		Increase prices		Outsource production	
RISKS	WEIGHT	SCORE	PTS	SCORE	PTS	SCORE	PTS
Market share loss to competition	10	7	*70*	10	*100*	3	*30*
Loss of retail shelf space	9	9	*81*	10	*90*	5	*45*
Loss of field sales support	8	8	*64*	10	*80*	4	*32*
Friction with upper management	9	10	*90*	2	*18*	7	*63*
Risk of late deliveries	7	1	*7*	1	*7*	10	*70*
Quality problem/image risk	9	1	*9*	0	*0*	10	*90*
TOTAL (ALL WEIGHTS)	52	*321*		*295*		*330*	
MAXIMUM POSSIBLE POINTS	*520*						
% OF MAXIMUM POINTS	*100%*	**62%**		**57%**		**63%**	

Capacity and marketing dilemma—Decision summary

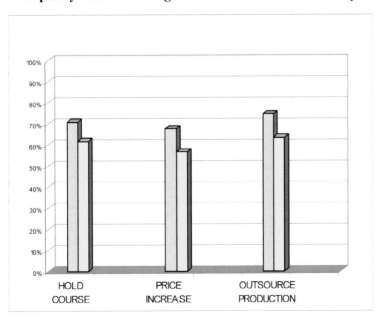

Conclusions—there were no good choices. Each alternative presented a "mixed bag" of positives and negatives that, on a weighted-fit basis, were about equal. Each demonstrated some reasonable (but not high) degree of fit with goals but each had high levels of risk. The product team was not happy with any of these choices and needed to find a better path.

A meeting at the production facility was scheduled immediately. There wasn't much time. The team would have to respond to upper management pressures shortly. And, if outsourcing were to be the answer, vendors would have to be engaged quickly or sales opportunities for the year would be lost.

After a plant tour, the team and plant management sat down for an informal discussion. The plant manager was under a lot of pressure and presented a litany of issues and complaints. Among many, one major frustration stood out: too much effort was being expended on complicated, high-end specialty products with low volume. These were part of a line of products always considered a strategic necessity by the Company. They were thought of as "image" products, and critical to maintaining a strong position against one high-end domestic competitor.

The production dynamics were unusual for this otherwise high-volume plant.

1. *These products were complicated and harder to produce.*
2. *The pre-production "set up" process was tedious and expensive.*
3. *Because annual volumes were low, the only efficient approach was to run the entire year's requirements with each production run.*
4. *This created an inventory bulge that always lasted for at least 12 months—creating a "physical turnover" of less than 1X.*
5. *Even with high profit margins, the high average inventory investment generated a poor ROI.*

A new idea was forming. The team asked how much incremental capacity might be generated if this entire line of specialty products were eliminated. This was considered a radical thought as these products had always been considered strategic—a "sacred cow" to be left untouched. The plant manager had a gleam in his eye as he did some quick calculations. In the end he estimated that capacity would be increased by over 25% if these resources were transferred entirely to high-volume production of core products.

The product manager promised to see what he could do. If these specialty products produced a substandard ROI for the business, they probably did the same for the relevant competitor. Why not "give away" the business if it would serve to improve market share in more important segments where the Company faced stronger competition. Adding this alternative to the matrix changed the picture entirely.

Capacity & marketing dilemma—Decision matrix II

Alternatives →		Hold current course		Increase prices		Outsource		Exit specialty	
GOALS	WT	SCORE	PTS	SCORE	PTS	SCORE	PTS	SCORE	PTS
Maximize profit margins	10	7	70	10	100	5	50	7	70
Maximize ROI	8	6	48	7	56	5	40	10	80
Maximize sales & mkt share	9	5	45	4	36	9	81	10	90
Maintain field sales morale	6	5	30	3	18	8	48	10	60
Maintain customer loyalty	7	7	49	3	21	10	70	9	63
Optimize plant utilization	5	6	30	7	35	5	25	10	50
TOTAL (ALL WEIGHTS)	45	272		266		314		413	
MAX. POSSIBLE POINTS	450								
% OF MAXIMUM POINTS	100%	60%		59%		70%		92%	

Capacity & marketing dilemma—Decision matrix II (cont'd)

Alternatives →		Hold current course		Increase prices		Outsource		Exit specialty	
RISKS	WEIGHT	SCORE	PTS	SCORE	PTS	SCORE	PTS	SCORE	PTS
Core segment loss to comp.	10	8	80	10	100	4	40	0	0
Specialty segment loss	3	0	0	3	9	0	0	10	30
Loss of retail shelf space	9	9	81	10	90	5	45	0	0
Loss of field sales support	8	8	64	10	80	4	32	1	8
Friction with upper mgt.	9	10	90	2	18	7	63	1	9
Risk of late deliveries	7	2	14	2	14	10	70	1	7
Quality & image risks	9	1	9	0	0	10	90	3	27
TOTAL (ALL WEIGHTS)	55	338		311		340		81	
MAX. POSSIBLE POINTS	550								
% OF MAXIMUM POINTS	100%	61%		57%		62%		15%	

Capacity & marketing dilemma—Decision summary II

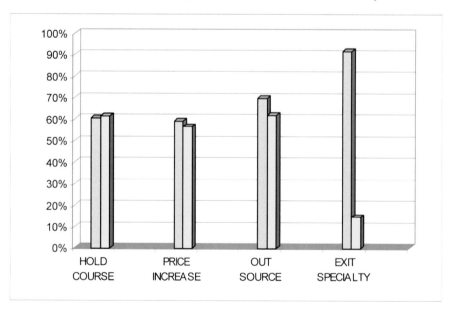

The weighted criteria stayed the same. The scoring of alternatives was affected to some degree by the inclusion of a fourth option (note: all rows must be re-scored when the number of alternatives is changed to reflect new comparisons). The value of adding a creative alternative was—in this case—dramatic, with a 92% fit with goals and a risk level of only 15%.

Results—the benefits of exiting the specialty product segment were so significant that the team had no problem gaining approval from senior management. Even those who would normally defend a sacred cow were hesitant to argue with the wisdom of this move. The sales force was ecstatic to learn that production and inventory for the most popular products would be increased dramatically and that prices would not be raised. The increase in volume and elimination of specialty manufacturing increased plant productivity—from the "worst" to "best" facility in less than one year—and lowered costs for all products produced. The bottom line was higher profits and increased market share in key growth segments. The only loser was one competitor who had been "handed" a larger share of an unprofitable segment.

In the Introduction, I referred to using the decision matrix to make a product design choice. The following is a similar use but refers to a "product concept" decision involving design and features. It is another example of the value of seeking creative alternatives to ensure the most optimal decision. In this case, the process led to the creation of a near-legendary product. The specifics have been modified slightly to protect confidential information.

Case number four—a new product decision. *A new product manager for GE radio products was asked to "sign off" on a new FM/AM portable radio concept. A two-year development cycle would ensue. This was to be a mid-range product targeted to retail for $49.95 and to compete at that price point with strong products from Panasonic and Sony. The product team generally accepted that Sony (in particular) had done a better job with "fit, finish, and design" and also had slightly superior sound quality compared to the older GE model. Competing with the Sony product was considered the primary goal. The proposed design concept had more modern styling, featured slightly better performance, and incorporated some more elegant parts and materials. Overall it was a good step forward but was slightly more expensive than its predecessor and would have somewhat lower profitability. Nevertheless, it was considered a competitive necessity.*

Consumer research (with brand names removed) confirmed that the new design would indeed compete on a par with the targeted Sony product. Although positive, this result still made the product manager uneasy. It was known that the Sony name was highly respected by retailers and consumers and perhaps the new model would not be received as superior with brand names revealed in the real marketplace. Furthermore, there was always a good chance that Sony would develop a new and better model at the same time—creating a moving target that would be invisible until market introduction. In the end, the model that GE would face might well be better than the current competitive offering.

As a starting point, the product manager used the decision matrix to compare three models (current model, new concept, current Sony model). This would be set up as a hypothetical circumstance to compare the three radios as if they were all part of the same product line. The results were not encouraging.

Competitive comparison—Decision matrix I

Alternatives →		Current model		New design concept		Sony model	
GOALS	WEIGHT	SCORE	PTS	SCORE	PTS	SCORE	PTS
Competitive styling	10	5	50	9	90	10	100
Competitive features	8	6	48	8	64	10	80
Competitive performance	7	7	49	10	70	9	63
Good cost/profit margins	8	9	72	7	56	10	80
Retail trade acceptance	9	4	36	8	72	10	90
Brand image enhancement	6	3	18	8	48	10	60
TOTAL (ALL WEIGHTS)	48	273		400		473	
MAX. POSSIBLE POINTS	480						
% OF MAXIMUM POINTS	100%	57%		83%		99%	

Competitive comparison—Decision matrix I (cont'd)

Alternatives →		Current model		New design concept		Sony model	
RISKS	WEIGHT	SCORE	PTS	SCORE	PTS	SCORE	PTS
Failure in the marketplace	10	10	*100*	5	*50*	1	*10*
TOTAL (ALL WEIGHTS)	10	*100*		*50*		*10*	
MAX. POSSIBLE POINTS	*100*						
% OF MAXIMUM POINTS	*100%*	**100%**		**50%**		**10%**	

This matrix served to demonstrate the necessity of replacing the then-current model, but also quantified reasons to be nervous about the new concept—i.e., would it become a "me too" product that didn't quite measure up? For comparison purposes, it was assumed that the Sony model had some offshore manufacturing cost advantages and was a good image product for them. It was a tough competitive target.

The only risk considered was a big one—the possibility of failure in the marketplace following a two-year development effort. This risk was magnified by the likelihood that Sony might introduce a new product in the same time frame at the same price point.

There had to be a better answer. The product manager called a meeting of the design engineering and industrial design teams. The challenge was to find a better idea. The meeting lasted three hours. In retrospect, this meeting would turn out to be worth approximately $15 million per hour—a number based on future sales of the "radical concept" that came out of the session. In short, the idea was to take an inexpensive printed circuit board chassis from another product line, convert it for use in a two-way power portable (battery and AC), and build up the performance with a massive speaker and high-end antenna system. The idea was that the savings in the FM/AM chassis might more than pay for the more expensive speakers and antennae. No one in the meeting knew if this was feasible. Considered "folly" by some on the team, the concept was handed over to advanced engineering for evaluation.

Under significant time pressures, the advanced engineering group prototyped and tested the idea. The results were startling. The concept was dramatically superior to any product in the line. It exhibited several strong characteristics.

1. *It had superior long-range reception due to the antenna system (in spite of the minimalist chassis).*

2. *It had vastly superior sound quality due to a very heavy magnet speaker (larger than any in the industry at that time).*

3. *It had very low battery drain due to the small chassis. This would give the product very long "battery life."*

4. *The space saved by the small chassis would put more "air" behind the massive speaker which further enhanced sound quality.*

5. *The net savings in terms of parts and materials would make this product exceptionally profitable at the intended price point. Note: little money would be spent on elegant appearances; it would all go to performance.*

Including this radical new concept in the competitive matrix changed the picture completely.

Competitive comparison—Decision matrix II

Alternatives →		Current model		New design concept		Sony model		Radical concept	
GOALS	WEIGHT	SCORE	PTS	SCORE	PTS	SCORE	PTS	SCORE	PTS
Competitive styling	10	5	50	9	90	10	100	8	80
Competitive features	8	6	48	8	64	10	80	9	72
Competitive performance	7	4	28	6	42	5	35	10	70
Good cost/profit margins	8	7	56	6	48	8	64	10	80
Retail trade acceptance	9	3	27	6	54	7	63	10	90
Brand image enhancement	6	3	18	6	36	8	48	10	60
TOTAL (ALL WEIGHTS)	48	227		334		390		452	
MAX. POSSIBLE POINTS	480								
% OF MAXIMUM POINTS	100%	47%		70%		81%		94%	

Competitive comparison—Decision matrix II (cont'd)

Alternatives →		Current model		New design concept		Sony model		Radical concept	
RISKS	WEIGHT	SCORE	PTS	SCORE	PTS	SCORE	PTS	SCORE	PTS
Failure in the marketplace	10	10	*100*	8	*80*	6	*60*	2	*20*
TOTAL (ALL WEIGHTS)	10	*100*		*80*		*60*		*20*	
MAX. POSSIBLE POINTS	*100*								
% OF MAXIMUM POINTS	*100%*	**100%**		**80%**		**60%**		**20%**	

Competitive comparison—Decision summary

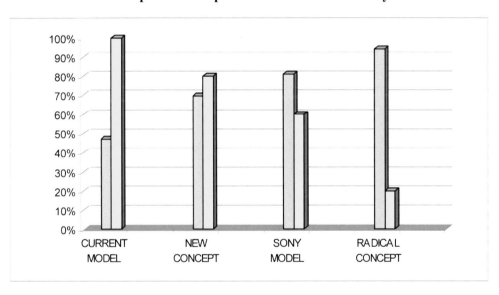

The product manager could now move ahead with a high level of confidence and the enthusiastic support of top management. The product was later announced to the trade as the "Superadio" and exceeded all expectations. Retail clerks were so impressed they began switching customers away from high-end Sony and Panasonic products. Everyone in the sales force had one at home. Young people bought it for the "big sound" capabilities. Older couples bought it for the long range performance in isolated "second homes." It sold well over a million units at high profit margins. It reestablished

market share dominance for GE in portable radios and became the cornerstone of a line of higher-performance models that followed.

Observation—it is still possible to create a $50 million business in one meeting. Sometimes it is just a matter of finding a more creative alternative.

Chapter VIII

SEQUENTIAL DECISIONS

Eliminating alternatives in a series of decisions. Sometimes an important decision can be finalized in one step. Other times it is beneficial to approach it in two or more steps, condensing the list of alternatives each time. Those with the highest relative merit are extracted from the entire list and then matched against one another. It is similar to a championship playoff series and is a typical sequence for most key hiring decisions (see Chapter X). It is also typical of the screening process used by investment firms of all types. I have chosen a venture capital group to show how this might work.

As the list of alternatives is condensed, the decision criteria are unchanged but the "relative scoring" is affected. The purpose of this chapter is to familiarize the reader with the mathematical consequences of condensing the number of alternatives in a sequential process. Understanding the numerical dynamics will help all users know how to interpret results. In general, the weighted fit with goals for each alternative will likely change very little while the relative risk levels will appear to increase; sometimes dramatically. The example presented below will explain why this happens, what to expect, and how to deal with it.

Key process note—there is no practical limit to the number of alternatives that can be effectively considered. **A high number makes the scoring more time-consuming but will not distort or dilute results** as would be the case with large numbers of goals and risks (note: I have used the matrix to consider as many as twenty alternatives at one time). Eliminating the weaker ones sequentially will condense the list logically, produce a more manageable group, and help to refine final considerations. Each time the list of alternatives is reduced, all relative scoring must be reconsidered; starting with the first line, assigning or reassigning the 10 and progressing from there. For purposes of space, the following case is limited to the second step of a sequential decision wherein the candidates have been reduced to five. Note: the following example is based on real companies but with hypothetical names and modified details. The data and assessments presented should not reflect on any existing companies and any resemblance is strictly coincidental. The process is the key point.

Case number five—venture capital investment decision. *A prominent Boston-based venture capital company had recently raised a new fund of over $1 billion and allocated 10% to startup or early-stage companies. The balance was reserved for post second-round and pre-IPO investments. After initial presentations, due diligence, and follow up meetings, the partners had reduced the number of near-term investment candidates to five. The purpose of this example is to show how the decision matrix is impacted by the sequential narrowing of choices. The thumbnail sketches of the candidate companies have been abbreviated to keep the focus on the process.*

Logistics, Inc.

This company was the brainchild of an M.I.T. professor who had developed a new algorithm for optimizing physical logistics for companies with operations around the world. The product was based on proprietary software developed by a team of software engineers and a handful of graduate students. The Company had utilized "seed capital" to develop their product, test its viability, and apply for patent protection. They now needed more substantial investment to establish a corporate site, develop the full operational team, and begin initial sales and marketing efforts. They had a unique product with strong profit and growth potential with significant barriers to competition. The founders also had intentions to sell the technology in two to three years thus offering the prospect of an early cash-out for investors. However, they did not have any proven managerial or marketing expertise in the team.

Retail, Inc.

RI was formed by an experienced group of software professionals and former retail executives. Their software system was designed to help management optimize pricing, merchandising, and inventory decisions in very competitive retail environments with short profit margins. The potential market was very large and potential profits look promising. There were some concerns about how well the product could be protected but this was pretty much a "given" in software designed for corporations—it could come from in-house development or other packaged software vendors. As a consequence, the management team was very realistic about "valuation" and was receptive to attractive terms for investors. They wanted to get started aggressively.

Medical, Inc.

MI was formed by two professors from Harvard to build diagnostic testing methods for the detection of cancer cells. They were highly-regarded in academic circles as leading-edge thinkers and were experienced project managers. There was a high level of confidence that their proprietary technology could be protected. They were not, however, savvy about marketing or strategic partnerships with "third parties." They also put a very high valuation on the Company. Nevertheless, they were extremely bright, had high profit expectations, and would be opportunistic about cashing out in three to four years.

E-bank, Inc.

E-bank was formed by a group of experienced executives with proven marketing and strategic planning skills. The software was designed to provide a simplified but more powerful consumer tool for electronic banking. The business plan and presentations were convincing in terms of consumer appeal and the size of the market in future years. The product was very impressive but it was not clear that competitive barriers would be high. In addition, there were some reservations about how much follow-on investment might be required to support a competitive marketing campaign. There were also some concerns about the potential for conflicting egos at the top. Nevertheless, the initial investment required was minimal, the management team was excellent, and a winning product would be very valuable.

Automotive, Inc.

This company was formed by a small group of retired executives and engineers from the "big three" in Detroit. They had pooled their own seed money to develop a proprietary "chip" that had the potential to improve fuel economy for all fuel-injected engines. The potential improvements were incrementally small but could become extremely valuable on a large scale. Any company that could successfully impact fuel economy would become a major "hit" and would be worth several hundred million dollars if not more. However, it would not be an easy sell into a tough industry and there would be heavy competitive development in many forms. In addition, the potential "battle of egos" was apparent in previous meetings and a cause for some concern. Nevertheless, the sheer magnitude of potential put this firm among the top five contenders for investment.

The venture fund partners held several long meetings to discuss the relative merits of these early stage companies. The discussions focused mostly on the management teams or founders but also included product concept potential, competitive barriers, cash-out potential, and an overall sense of the "odds." Some partners were willing to narrow the list or make a decision based on "chemistry" with the prospect company founders while others wanted to "scrub" the numbers in order to make a colder assessment of potential.

There was no consensus around the table—they were dealing with diverse technologies in different industries. In order to put some structure into the decision, the group decided to develop a standard set of investment criteria they could use for this and subsequent decisions of a similar nature. Their plan was to refine the criteria over time and use them to compare (1) any group of new investment opportunities, (2) existing investments vs. new candidates, (3) successful past investments vs. new opportunities, or (4) modified alternatives that were previously eliminated.

The first application of these new criteria was to compare the five investment candidates outlined above. The results helped to move the process forward with minimal debate.

VC investment alternatives—Decision matrix

Alternatives →	WT	Logistics, Inc. SCORE	PTS	Retail, Inc. SCORE	PTS	Medical, Inc. SCORE	PTS	E-Bank, Inc. SCORE	PTS	Auto, Inc. SCORE	PTS
GOALS	WT	SCORE	PTS	SCORE	PTS	SCORE	PTS	SCORE	PTS	SCORE	PTS
Management team	10	6	60	8	80	10	100	9	90	5	50
Proprietary technology	8	10	80	7	56	9	72	4	32	9	72
Industry growth potential	5	8	40	8	40	10	50	6	30	8	40
Marketing expertise	8	4	32	7	56	6	48	10	80	8	64
Profit potential	7	10	70	8	56	9	63	3	21	4	28
Cash-out time frame	5	10	50	7	35	8	40	4	20	5	25
Reasonable evaluation	7	7	49	10	70	5	35	7	49	5	35
Limited Investment required	6	8	48	5	30	7	42	8	48	10	60
TOTAL (ALL WEIGHTS)	56	429		423		450		370		374	
MAX. POSSIBLE POINTS	560										
% OF MAXIMUM POINTS	100%	77%		76%		80%		66%		67%	

VC investment alternatives—Decision matrix (cont'd)

Alternatives →	WT	Logistics, Inc.		Retail, Inc.		Medical, Inc.		E-Bank, Inc.		Auto, Inc.	
RISKS	WT	SCORE	PTS	SCORE	PTS	SCORE	PTS	SCORE	PTS	SCORE	PTS
New competitive threats	10	3	30	8	80	5	50	10	100	9	90
2nd best technology	7	4	28	5	35	4	28	9	63	10	70
Sales & marketing failure	8	4	32	3	24	5	40	8	64	10	80
Major follow-on investment	8	6	48	6	48	5	40	10	80	8	64
Political infighting/morale	4	3	12	4	16	4	16	7	28	10	40
Customer support failure	5	2	10	6	30	2	10	8	40	10	50
TOTAL (ALL WEIGHTS)	42	160		233		184		375		394	
MAX. POSSIBLE POINTS	420										
% OF MAXIMUM POINTS	100%	38%		55%		44%		89%		94%	

VC investment alternatives—Decision summary

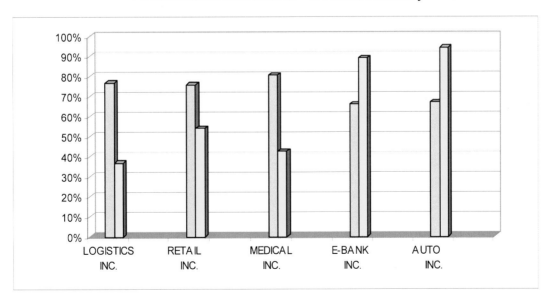

What might have been felt instinctively in some minds was now made clear; there were just too many risks with E-bank and Automotive. They were quickly ruled out and the matrix was rerun to see how the top three would score when measured only against one another. This sharpened the picture.

VC investment alternatives—Decision matrix II

Alternatives →		Logistics, Inc.		Retail, Inc.		Medical, Inc.	
GOALS	WT	SCORE	PTS	SCORE	PTS	SCORE	PTS
Management team	10	6	60	8	80	10	100
Proprietary technology	8	10	80	7	56	9	72
Industry growth potential	5	8	40	8	40	10	50
Marketing expertise	8	5	40	10	80	9	72
Profit potential	7	10	70	8	56	9	63
Cash-out time frame	5	10	50	7	35	8	40
Reasonable evaluation	7	7	49	10	70	5	35
Limited Investment required	6	10	60	6	36	9	54
TOTAL (ALL WEIGHTS)	56	449		453		486	
MAX. POSSIBLE POINTS	560						
% OF MAXIMUM POINTS	100%	80%		81%		87%	

Alternatives →		Logistics, Inc.		Retail, Inc.		Medical, Inc.	
RISKS	WT	SCORE	PTS	SCORE	PTS	SCORE	PTS
New competitive threats	10	4	40	10	100	6	60
2nd best technology	7	3	21	10	70	3	21
Sales & marketing failure	8	8	64	6	48	10	80
Major follow-on investment	8	10	80	9	72	7	56
Political infighting/morale	4	5	20	9	36	10	40
Customer support failure	5	3	15	10	50	3	15
TOTAL (ALL WEIGHTS)	42	240		376		272	
MAX. POSSIBLE POINTS	420						
% OF MAXIMUM POINTS	100%	57%		90%		65%	

VC investment alternatives—Decision summary

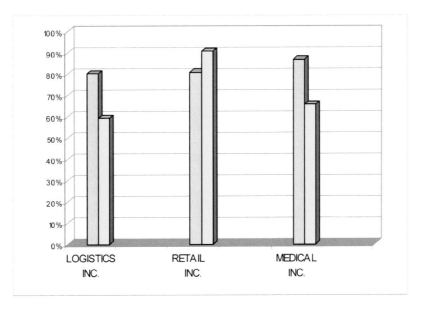

Observation—while the fit with goals totals increased slightly for all three prospects, the associated risk scores increased significantly. This occurred for two reasons. The first was associated with the case itself. Startup companies are inherently risky. Any rational assessment of risk will show why—there are always many unknowns and it is a very competitive world.

The second reason is more important and has to do with simple math. Because the two alternatives with the highest risk levels were removed, the "10-point rule" will force assignment of higher relative risk onto the three remaining. Remember, they are not being measured in an absolute sense but only compared to each other. Note that the same effect is rarely seen in terms of fit with goals and objectives; the winners are usually the ones having the highest positive scores to begin with, and little is gained by elimination of the weaker choices.

The venture partners now looked at their two leading candidates, Logistics, Inc. and Medical, Inc. They realized that both companies had strong positive attributes but also carried risk. They also recognized that positives and negatives were being measured on different scales. Nevertheless, they studied the de-

tail to see if there were ways to enhance strengths or reduce weaknesses for the more heavily weighted (more important) factors associated with each company.

Medical, Inc. was strong across the board on all important objectives. The largest risks were political infighting potential and the possibility of failing to market their systems effectively. There were no solid ideas about how to minimize either risk at that time.

The weaknesses with Logistics, Inc. were related to the management team, marketing expertise (both in the goals criteria), risk of industry partnership failures, and the need for follow-on investment. If a strong CEO, backed by an experienced VP of marketing could be found and hired, the partners felt certain this would be a very good investment and that other venture funds would be willing to participate in initial and follow-on investments. They were confident they could persuade the founder to become chairman and spokesperson for the Company and to leave operations to an experienced team. They decided to rerun the matrix with these assumptions in place. The results were impacted in very positive ways.

VC investment alternatives—Decision matrix III

Alternatives →		Logistics, Inc.		Retail, Inc.		Medical, Inc.	
GOALS	WT	SCORE	PTS	SCORE	PTS	SCORE	PTS
Management team	10	9	*90*	8	*80*	10	*100*
Proprietary technology	8	10	*80*	7	*56*	9	*72*
Industry growth potential	5	8	*40*	8	*40*	10	*50*
Marketing expertise	8	8	*64*	10	*80*	9	*72*
Profit potential	7	10	*70*	8	*56*	9	*63*
Cash-out time frame	5	10	*50*	7	*35*	8	*40*
Reasonable evaluation	7	7	*49*	10	*70*	5	*35*
Limited Investment required	6	10	*60*	6	*36*	9	*54*
TOTAL (ALL WEIGHTS)	56	*503*		*453*		*486*	
MAX. POSSIBLE POINTS	*560*						
% OF MAXIMUM POINTS	*100%*	*90%*		*81%*		*87%*	

VC investment alternatives—Decision matrix III (cont'd)

Alternatives →		Logistics, Inc.		Retail, Inc.		Medical, Inc.	
RISKS	WT	SCORE	PTS	SCORE	PTS	SCORE	PTS
New competitive threats	10	4	40	10	100	6	60
2nd best technology	7	3	21	10	70	3	21
Sales & marketing failure	8	3	24	6	48	10	80
Major follow-on investment	8	6	48	10	80	6	48
Political infighting/morale	4	5	20	9	36	10	40
Customer support failure	5	3	15	10	50	3	15
TOTAL (ALL WEIGHTS)	42	*168*		*384*		*264*	
MAX. POSSIBLE POINTS	420						
% OF MAXIMUM POINTS	*100%*	**40%**		**91%**		**63%**	

VC investment alternatives—Decision summary

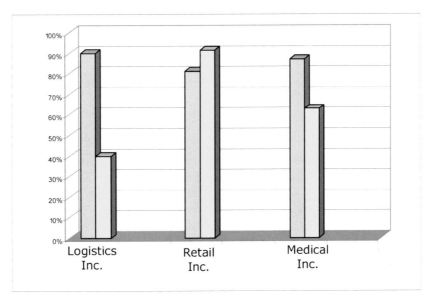

The partners decided to make an investment in Logistics, Inc. contingent on the Company's attraction of a CEO and marketing vice president with solid performance records.

Compressing the number of alternatives will always have this effect. No matter how long or short the risk criteria are, or how they are weighted, risk levels will appear to rise. It works in the opposite way as well—expanding the number of alternatives will always reduce the *apparent relative risk* for better alternatives. There is no impact on mathematical integrity: remember that these are assessments of *relative risk* and not *absolute risk.*

Taken to the extreme, it would seem that compressing the alternatives down to only one would inexorably drive the risk level to 100% against any criteria. This, of course, is not the case and brings us to the concept of *testing* any answer.

Finding optimal answers. What seems like a mathematical peculiarity is actually a strength. It serves to put a major decision-making dilemma on the table. How do you know when the best choice among alternatives is good enough? How do you know that the best alternative you have been able to identify will not lead you down the path to mediocrity?

I have not found any evidence that traditional decision theory addresses this issue. And yet, at the end of every decision process, there comes a moment when you or your company must choose a course of action. Knowing that you have identified the best choice among many is a good start. Knowing that you have found a choice that will measure up in an absolute sense is better. This should always be your goal—not to find better answers but to find *optimal answers.*

Previous chapters have demonstrated the method and value of modifying alternatives or finding better, more creative alternatives. In the next chapter, we will take the matrix in a new direction, using it to measure the absolute or *intrinsic merit* of any alternative

Chapter IX

TESTING FOR INTRINSIC MERIT

When is good, good enough? No matter how you have sorted out all imaginative and viable alternatives, there is always one question that remains. Is the best of these alternatives good enough? Will it measure up to expectations? Will it be successful?

This issue can be thought of in several ways.

- Absolute merit or strength when considered alone.
- Instrinsic merit as opposed to relative merit.
- Relative merit when compared to a fixed benchmark.

It is a test—a way to *benchmark* the strength of any chosen path. Sometimes the best from a group is not good enough. This is especially true if the criteria were less than comprehensive or the alternatives did not include new ideas. In either case, you can pick the best of the lot and still end up with a poor choice.

How would you know? The purpose of this chapter is to use the decision matrix in a slightly different way to provide this final test.

Establishing a benchmark. Chapter VIII addressed the mathematical certainties that occur when the number of alternatives is condensed or expanded. The principle is worth repeating.

- Condensing the number of alternatives may slightly alter the relative goal fit but will significantly increase the levels of apparent risk. This occurs as relative risk is shifted from eliminated alternatives to those remaining.

- In reverse, expanding the number of alternatives may slightly alter the relative goal fit but will likely reduce the levels of apparent risk for the stronger alternatives. This happens as risk is shifted to the weaker options.

Even with a static number of alternatives, the measures of weighted fit are still only relative comparisons. Hence, there is often a necessity to test the final answer against some standard to determine intrinsic excellence—the inherent benefits and risks of any single choice.

The process is quite simple. You begin with the same criteria that were developed to sort out alternatives. These are, after all, your best lists of goals and risks carefully weighted for importance. To illustrate the point, I will use the criteria from the last chapter as developed by the venture capital firm.

Venture capital—Investment criteria

POSITIVE CRITERIA	
OBJECTIVES	WEIGHT
Management team	10
Proprietary technology	8
Industry growth potential	5
Marketing expertise	8
Profit potential	7
Cash-out time frame	5
Reasonable evaluation	7
Limited Investment required	6
TOTAL (ALL WEIGHTS)	56

NEGATIVE CRITERIA	
RISKS	WEIGHT
New competitive threats	10
2nd best technology	7
Sales & marketing failure	8
Major follow-on investment	8
Political infighting/morale	4
Customer support failure	5
TOTAL (ALL WEIGHTS)	42

Key process note—these are exactly as used to compare investment alternatives. It is important that they not be changed for this step. If there is a refinement that would improve the criteria, you need to back up one step, modify the matrix, and re-measure all alternatives against it. Then you are ready to move ahead.

In the next step, the best investment alternative from the last chapter is measured against these criteria on its own. In one sense, it will still be a relative score—i.e. how close this one alternative comes to being a perfect fit.

Key process note—when scoring an individual alternative against the criteria, you may use 10 as many times as you deem it appropriate. A 10 for every goal and a 0 for every risk would generate a perfect score (100% and 0% respectively). No such scoring is possible but many excellent choices will get close. Here's what the scoring might look like for the leading alternative from the investment example.

Investment decision—Benchmark test

Candidate →		Logistics, Inc.		Notes
GOALS	WT	SCORE	PTS	
Management team	10	9	*90*	Very strong with key executive additions.
Proprietary technology	8	10	*80*	Very strong with good patent potential.
Industry growth potential	5	9	*45*	Very high given global economic conditions.
Marketing expertise	8	8	*64*	Very high with key executive hire.
Profit potential	7	9	*63*	Very high potential value to corporate customers.
Cash-out time frame	5	10	*50*	Very solid short term exit strategy.
Reasonable evaluation	7	8	*56*	High profit and ROI potential.
Investment requirements	6	10	*60*	Relatively small $ and good partnership potential.
TOTAL (ALL WEIGHTS)	56	*508*		**91%**
MAX. POSSIBLE PTS.	*560*			
% OF MAXIMUM PTS.	*100%*	**91%**		

Investment decision—Benchmark test (cont'd)

Candidate →		Logistics, Inc.		Notes
RISKS	WT	SCORE	PTS	
New competitive threats	10	2	*20*	Low risk given advanced nature of technology.
2nd best technology	7	2	*14*	Low risk given industry stature of inventor.
Sales & marketing failure	8	3	*24*	Low probability based on new CEO and VP of Mktg.
Major follow-on investment	8	2	*16*	Strong investor partnerships expected.
Political infighting/morale	4	3	*12*	Improved with changes in the mgt. team.
Customer support failure	5	2	*10*	Readily available talent for expanding quality support.
TOTAL (ALL WEIGHTS)	42	*96*		**23%**
MAX. POSSIBLE PTS.	*420*			
% OF MAXIMUM PTS.	*100%*	*23%*		

Key process note—once in a while an alternative will receive a zero for any given risk. However, this will be extremely rare. Even the slightest level of risk will deserve a score of one or higher. If an alternative was so risk-free as to receive a score of 1 for each risk in the matrix, it would inexorably generate a total risk level of 10%. For all practical purposes, **10% should be considered a realistic minimum in any risk matrix**. The investment choice in the example above is estimated to have a 23% risk factor. This may be 23% above the *theoretical minimum* but is only 13% above the realistic minimum of ten percent. Keep this in mind as you interpret results. If 10% is the floor, then this decision might be looked at as a 91%-13% fit. These are strong numbers.

Interpreting the numbers. How do you know when you are looking at an adequate score? At first glance this might seem difficult but it is not. There are several ways to interpret results on a consistent basis.

1. Use the author's guidelines as a starting point.
2. Test criteria fit for your own past successes and failures.
3. Combine elements from past decisions to build theoretical composite benchmarks.
4. Track your results over time to establish company standards.

As a starting point, I can say with confidence that any alternative demonstrating an 85% to 90% fit with goals is probably a strong choice. On the risk side, any alternative scoring 25% to 30% is usually good. Keep in mind that these numbers are neither additive nor reciprocal. They are independent assessments and must be judged accordingly. A very aggressive benchmark would be 90% and 15% respectively.

Any alternative with a legitimate score of over 90% will almost always be a winner as long as risk levels are modest—hence the title of this book. **90% is the *gold standard*** and you may want to aim for it; especially with very important decisions. You might settle for 85% if the decision is not critical, there are no other creative alternatives, or there is no viable way to improve the leading alternative. You might also relax the acceptable risk level for similar reasons.

A good way to test this assumption is to take a successful decision from your company's history and run it through the matrix. If you were the venture capital investment company in the last example, you might want to compare one or two successful investments from the past to one you are considering now. Using a consistent matrix for the comparison should provide a good benchmark and an immediate answer.

For another example of the same principle, assume you hired a new manager of engineering two years ago and he has performed extremely well. Develop a matrix for this position (as if you were about to make the decision again) and see how he would have measured up. If you do this for several successful people, you will begin to see a pattern. It should change very little with repeated testing or experience over time. You can also do the reverse. Build a matrix for a position that is "open." Objectively score the previous office occupant. If he was a great performer, you will have a sense of what would be a good profile for the next candidate. If he was mediocre or an outright failure, you will have a good sense of a profile to avoid. Either way, you should be able to zero in on a solid set of benchmarks in a short period of time. Note that the absolute numbers will not be as important as looking for *equivalency*—a new choice that is as good as or better than a successful one from the past.

A third approach is to combine the best of two or more. Continuing with the personnel example, let's assume you are hiring a new VP of marketing. If the last two vice presidents were quite successful but had different strengths and weaknesses, you might combine the best of both to see how strong this hypothetical composite would look against the matrix. This would probably *set the bar* fairly high but it would give you a good sense of the upper end of the range. Any single new candidate who approached this hypothetical profile would probably be an excellent choice.

No matter where you begin, patterns should begin to emerge quickly and remain consistent over time. In a cooperative environment, these can become *standards* by which all decisions are measured. If you can reach this point, all collective decisions will be improved and will take less time to achieve. See Chapter XII for more discussion on this aspect.

As you develop personal or corporate standards, keep in mind that they may vary for different decisions.

1. They may be tighter for more important decisions than for those of lesser consequence.
2. They may be different for different types of decisions—e.g. short term versus long term, large investment versus limited expense, or committed course versus reversible.
3. They may differ by business function or level.
4. They may be relaxed if a decision must be made now and a sub-optimal choice is better than waiting. This is always a dangerous path for important decisions but may be dictated by the clock. Don't do it unless you absolutely have to. And, think first about ways to reverse it quickly if it is not working.

In other words, you may develop sets of benchmarks as opposed to a single benchmark. Tailoring benchmarks in this fashion will make the decision process faster and more effective. You won't have to fight to hold every decision to the highest standards.

Personnel decisions are frequent and of obvious importance to the strength of any organization, top to bottom. They often spell the difference between an organization that can move quickly and compete effectively versus those that will always be second best. The decision matrix is not only a solid way to ensure good individual decisions but also to establish company-wide standards for excellence—standards that can make all hiring managers more effective.

The next case is used to show what happened when the choice for a new VP of sales was held to company benchmarks based on the matrix.

Case number six—a new vice president of sales. *A small high-tech company was in crisis mode. Their sales were falling under heavy competitive pressures and their VP of sales had recently left to join a non-competing entity. The regional managers were without a leader and the pressure to revive sales was severe. The CEO initiated an aggressive search through an executive recruiting firm that knew the Company well and also urged all members of the executive staff to use their own personal networks to seek out quality candidates as quickly as possible.*

Within four weeks, three high-potential candidates were identified. Any one of them might have been able to do the job but they were very different types of people.

Mr. Consultant
The first candidate was very bright, well-educated, and had a solid background in the management consulting industry. He had excellent communications and conceptual skills and a good grasp of relevant technologies. He was also dedicated to seeking out and providing comprehensive competitive analyses that could help the Company compete more effectively with emerging threats. He did not, however, have much experience with organization management or the forceful execution of a professional sales process. He understood the sales process but was not highly experienced in its implementation.

Mr. Personality
The second candidate was bright and congenial. He had in-depth sales experience and had very strong references from past customers and employers. He worked very hard and was liked by everyone he met. He also had a very good grasp of the technical aspects of the Company's products. On the other hand, his "people-management" credentials were modest in that he had never had national responsibilities. There was also a concern that he had not "closed" major sales contracts in the past without senior executive help.

Mr. Process
The third candidate was an aggressive, goal-oriented manager. He had a strong track record and excellent people-management skills. However, his technical and conceptual skills were modest compared to the other candidates. There was some concern that he might not become popular within the Company and might fracture some customer relationships along the way. Nevertheless, everyone was confident that he could generate the numbers the Company needed.

Comparing these three in the standard matrix produced the following results.

Sales Vice President—Decision matrix

Alternatives →		Mr. Consultant		Mr. Personality		Mr. Process	
GOALS	WT	SCORE	PTS	SCORE	PTS	SCORE	PTS
Good management skills	8	5	40	6	48	10	80
Strong sales process skills	9	4	36	6	54	10	90
Successful sales record	10	4	40	6	60	10	100
Technical knowledge	5	10	50	8	40	7	35
Communication skills	7	10	70	8	56	7	49
Conceptual abilities	5	10	50	7	35	5	25
Good addition to mgt team	5	10	50	7	35	8	40
Boost customer relations	4	6	24	10	40	4	16
Gather competitive intel.	5	10	50	6	30	3	15
TOTAL (ALL WEIGHTS)	58	410		398		450	
MAX. POSSIBLE POINTS	580						
% OF MAXIMUM POINTS	100%	71%		69%		78%	

Alternatives →		Mr. Consultant		Mr. Personality		Mr. Process	
RISKS	WT	SCORE	PTS	SCORE	PTS	SCORE	PTS
Fall short of sales targets	10	10	100	7	70	3	30
Fail to enable sales team	8	10	80	8	64	4	32
Damage customer rapport	4	2	8	1	4	10	40
Create internal friction	3	1	3	2	6	10	30
Risk proprietary assets	4	2	8	5	20	10	40
TOTAL (ALL WEIGHTS)	29	199		164		172	
MAX. POSSIBLE POINTS	290						
% OF MAXIMUM POINTS	100%	69%		57%		59%	

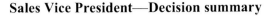

Sales Vice President—Decision summary

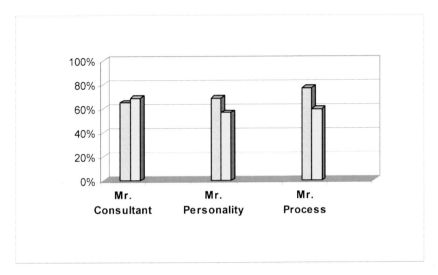

As is often the case, these candidates exhibited completely different profiles. The candidate with the consultancy background was the *polar opposite* of the aggressive process candidate. They had completely different strengths and weaknesses that, for the most part, balanced out. The most personable candidate fell somewhere in the middle with few strong points to recommend him. On the basis of overall weighted fit, Mr. Process had a slight edge.

Top management was ready to move ahead with the third and most aggressive candidate. The Company needed to generate revenue and this candidate had the strongest sales credentials. The CEO was impressed by his energy, management skills, and ability to generate sales. However, the VP of human resources cautioned him about organizational risks and the VP of software development was concerned about the lack of technical skills. He was the best of the three but would he be a smart choice?

The team elected to go the next step and compare this candidate to a benchmark for intrinsic merit. The top managers, as a group, scored the candidate line by line. When they were in agreement with each element, they moved on to the next. The matrix did the rest and the bottom line put a numerical face on their uneasy feelings.

Sales VP—Benchmark test

Candidate →		Mr. Process	
GOALS	WT	SCORE	PTS
Good management skills	8	10	80
Strong sales process skills	9	9	81
Successful sales record	10	9	90
Technical knowledge	5	7	35
Communication skills	7	6	42
Conceptual sales ability	5	6	30
Good addition to mgt team	5	6	30
Boost customer relations	4	4	16
Gather competitive intel.	5	3	15
TOTAL (ALL WEIGHTS)	58	419	
MAX. POSSIBLE POINTS	580		
% OF MAXIMUM POINTS	100%	72%	

Candidate →		Mr. Process	
RISKS	WT	SCORE	PTS
Fall short of sales targets	10	4	40
Fail to enable sales team	8	3	24
Damage customer rapport	4	7	28
Create internal friction	3	7	21
Risk proprietary assets	4	5	20
TOTAL (ALL WEIGHTS)	29	133	
MAX. POSSIBLE POINTS	290		
% OF MAXIMUM POINTS	100%	46%	

The results were not encouraging. Given the extreme urgency, the management team might have been willing to take the gamble with numbers like 80% - 30%. However, this was a key position and a critical decision. A mistake would cost valuable time and might even pose a threat to the Company's survival. Even though it was a tough decision, they decided to appoint an "acting manager of sales" and put a heavier burden on their regional managers until a stronger candidate could be found.

In the end, a solid VP was found who had all of the skills the Company was seeking without the risks that burdened the current alternatives. He scored 92%-21% against the same criteria. It turned out to be a very good decision. With effective leadership, the sales organization surpassed all revenue targets and regained market share leadership within two years.

A benchmark test such as this can make the difference between the <u>best relative choice</u> and the <u>best absolute choice</u>. It is extremely important to know the difference.

Chapter X

GROUP DECISION-MAKING

Almost every decision in business is a collective decision. Even in dictatorial environments, most decisions are made around a conference table with multi-functional inputs. It is curious that little of what is written about decision-making includes consideration of this reality; it is a constant issue in every large corporation.

Inclusion. While it is true that some business leaders are in a position to make decisions unilaterally, they rarely approach them in that fashion. Even the most confident executives like to gather the opinions of others when considering important actions. At one end of the spectrum are respected opinions that might contribute to the wisdom and shape of the choices at hand. At the other end are people who may have to execute the decision and the inclusion of their inputs will generally increase enthusiasm and teamwork for the effort that follows.

Complexity. Important decisions are becoming increasingly complex. For much of business history, important issues were largely driven by financial concerns and potential impact in domestic markets. Over several decades, the range of considerations has been expanded greatly and now, for most companies, covers a broad spectrum.

- Globalization
  - Competitors
  - Markets
  - Complexities—physical, legal, financial, and cultural
- Rapid technological evolution
- High-speed communications (often worldwide)
- Productivity (expanded from manufacturing to all operations)
- Legal liability in a more litigious world
- Key personnel attraction and retention
- Equal opportunity and minority rights
- Public relations

> ➢ Employee benefits
> ➢ Protection of intellectual property and proprietary data
> ➢ Physical security
> ➢ Shareholder actions and hostile takeovers
> ➢ Mergers, acquisitions, and divestitures

I am sure we could easily add to the list. As decisions become more complex, so also do the meetings to address them. This means a tendency to put more people *in the room* and to keep them there longer. No wonder Patrick Lencioni wrote *Death by Meeting* (Jossey-Bass, 2004). In this day and age, it seems that every function has a role in almost every decision.

Beyond the complexity of issues, there is a built-in complexity that comes from the human dynamics of a group discussion. While it is obvious that each business division or function will have a natural bias (lawyers with legal issues, CFOs with financial issues, etc.) there are more subtle conflicts at work.

The first of these might be a variable sense of urgency. Even though every manager should be concerned about current-year results, their functional sensitivities to the calendar can be very different. Consider the following generalities drawn from many years of participation and observation.

Functional time horizons

Functional manager	Primary	Secondary
General Manager or CEO	Current month, quarter, and fiscal year	Two to three year outlook
Finance	Current quarter and fiscal year	Patterns impacting next year
Sales	Current month	Fiscal year targets
Manufacturing	This week's output, productivity and quality	Five to ten year capacity
Engineering	Near-term project completion (in months)	Long term technical trends
Human Resources	Today's human crises and benefits cost containment	Long term organization strength
Strategic Planning	Tactical program impact over next two to three years	Five year strategic plans
Legal Counsel	Pending litigation and near-term legal issues	Long term impact of legislative trends

These differences are inexorable. Important decisions will always contain many facets: different functions will represent different disciplines, and functional responsibilities will impact each participant's timing priorities and concerns. If these are not enough to send meetings into endless circles and endless hours, there is one more factor that is strictly human—different personalities.

While I am certainly not an expert in the categorization or interpretation of personalities, I do believe I have probably seen them all. Some of the primary categories are listed below. I am sure readers will recognize a few.

Politicians—those who generally put the advancement of themselves and their careers above the achievements of the organization. They may behave in a manner that benefits some parts of the organization but *promotion* will always take precedence over the business. They win when other people lose. These types, of course, are ubiquitous and unavoidable. They are the opposites of team players.

Warriors—these types actually look forward to meetings and bring energy with them. Meetings give them chances to battle with other *Alphas* and prevail. A good skirmish gives them a sense of accomplishment and self worth. Whether they are beneficial or detrimental to the organization depends on whether they just enjoy the fight or are fighting to achieve something positive. Regardless, they are likely to silence the voices of the less combative.

Goal seekers—these are the ones who want to get results; to *put points on the board*. These are usually the ones who will step forward to take on additional responsibilities even if it means much more work. They are geared to success and are often willing to risk failure to achieve it.

Process people—these are the opposites of goal seekers. They are oriented to the rules: *how things should be done* as opposed to *what needs to get done*. They live under the assumption that a good process will lead to good results. On the beneficial side of the ledger, they often keep the group on a rational and ethical track. On the weak side, they are often obstructive and instinctively prefer the *status quo.*

Optimists and pessimists—everyone falls on this scale somewhere. Positions on the scale may vary from issue to issue, but the basic predisposition tends to remain constant. The optimists are much more likely to start initiatives and take risks. The pessimists will see the dark side of almost any issue or action and are likely to be obstructionists. If practical (not incessant dreamers or naysayers), both types can be valuable—they will show you both sides of any issue and help you fill out both halves of the matrix.

I am sure experts could expand and refine this list. However, the end point would be the same: there are many kinds of personalities that further complicate the inherent conflicts in any collaborative decision. Adding personalities to the mix shows why it can be so difficult to reach agreement as a group.

> ➢ Issue complexity
> ➢ Biased functional views
> ➢ Multiple time horizons
> ➢ <u>Multiple personality types</u>
> ➢ **Group decision challenge**

It is no wonder that meetings tend to go on *ad nauseam* and often without conclusion. Sometimes the CEO or highest-ranking executive becomes tired of the debate and accepts a convenient compromise. Just as often the issue is tabled for future consideration. The latter may be the most common form of *corporate gridlock*. It is also a phenomenon that favors the *status quo*—even when it is a very risky path.

Q: How can the decision matrix facilitate a group process?

A: It is simpler than you might think.

The fundamental advantage of the matrix approach is the way it breaks down the decision into its component parts. Consider the first example in this book addressing a *compensation structure* decision (Chapter V). There were initially 20 positive and negative goal elements and three alternatives with over 30 perceived advantages and disadvantages. This yields over 600 discussion points. In the typical group meeting, these points would be discussed in random fashion. Corporate goals would be mixed with advantages and disadvantages of different alternatives in no particular order. If you were to add the complexities of bias, timeframe mismatches, functional differences, and personalities, you might have thousands of conflicting thoughts.

To make matters worse, human instinct will usually cause each participant to start with a preferred answer and then attempt to justify it to the rest of the group. Very few managers are neutral or objective about any issue, especially if it affects them personally or their organizations in any way.

This produces an *ad hoc* process wherein each participant starts with a preferred answer and attempts to explain the advantages while others look for faults. This process is usually time-consuming, often heated, and normally leads to flawed decisions or no decisions at all. It rarely produces an optimal decision.

The matrix approach not only reverses the process but also *isolates* each element so that rational agreement is facilitated. In essence, the decision is dissected into its individual components. **Considering any decision in its totality is no longer the starting point but is reserved for the end of the process.**

For a group decision, these are the logical steps and why they should produce superior results.

1. *Make a list of goals*.
   Open the discussion with a free-wheeling list of possible objectives; what you would like to accomplish with this decision. Do not allow any discussion of potential actions or alternatives. Encourage any and all ideas—i.e., let people know that their job is to make sure that nothing important is left out. For clarity, save the discussion of risks for later.

2. *Condense the list*.
   Challenge the group to eliminate duplications, combine similar items, or broaden categories to reduce the number of stated goals. This is still an inclusive list—no one's thoughts have been repudiated. You have already set the stage for a cooperative effort.

3. *Choose the most important goal*.
   This will often take some serious discussion. It will be facilitated by the fact that you will only be looking for "one" and not trying to rank order priorities. Even if this takes some time, it is worth it. It will be the *linchpin* of the matrix and every decision group should have a clear understanding of high priorities.

4. *Compare relative importance*.
   While there will always be room for argument, the fact that you go *line by line* to determine importance versus the most important goal will greatly assist a rational result. You are, as a group, only assigning one number at a time. Once the group is *centered* on a collective number, it can be nudged up or down slightly until its relative importance is generally accepted. Ideally, everyone will have had a chance to refine the number so that no one has been left out.

5. *Check for overweighting.*

Because there is a natural tendency to overweight any objective important enough to make the list, it is important to ask participants to challenge the numbers. There are four ways to do this:

    a. Add up the numerical value for all assigned weights. See what percent of the total your most important goal will represent. If there are 50 total points, it will be 20% of the decision. If there are 100 points, it will only be 10% of the decision. You will have a good sense of whether this is strong enough.

    b. Similarly, convert each number to a percentage of the total to see what the collective importance of your most important goals will be. If a cluster of important goals will not have enough influence, go back and differentiate more.

    c. Combine the weights of your least important goals to see how few it takes to overpower your most important goal. If it doesn't take much, you have diluted your most important goal(s).

    d. Combine two of your more important (but secondary) goals to see if they dramatically overpower the most important goal(s).

Use one or more of these to force greater differentiation in goal weighting. This will help to create a more conclusive end result. Note: if you cannot logically differentiate any more, then leave them as they are. The objective is a rational set of criteria and not a forced ranking. Make sure the group does not expect mathematical precision or certitude. It is neither possible nor necessary. You are dealing with approximations. In the end, the weighted average approach will tend to compensate for less-than-perfect scoring. In addition, the group can always test the results against a reasonable benchmark—as presented in the last chapter—to expose a weak conclusion.

6. *Make a list of risks.*

As in Step 1, this should be an open exchange in which you are encouraging the entire group to be certain that every downside risk is listed. Every idea, no matter how brilliant or dubious, should be included.

7. *Condense the list.*

   This is the same process as in Step 2 above. While some risks will represent the *flip side* of stated goals, these should be kept to a minimum—you do not want to create a mirror image. Urge the group to look for negative consequences as an independent exercise.

8. *Choose the most important risk.*

   Assign a 10 with same process as in Step 3 above. Stay with this until there is unanimous agreement.

9. *Compare relative importance.*

   In this case, you are assessing the real potential for negative impact on the business. Do not gloss over this section. It may provide the key to an optimal decision later. Check for overweighting as in Step 5 above.

   At this point, you should be standing on firm ground. You have a solid basis for consideration of any alternative. The fact that this framework will stay fixed while the group considers alternatives forces a sequence that will vastly improve results—i.e., goals, risks, and alternatives will never be mixed together.

   At this point, you may notice something new happening around the table. The most aggressive participants, or those who are accustomed to winning, will start to worry about where the decision is headed. It won't do them much good—it is very hard to project an outcome and to preempt a rational end result.

   You may also notice that those whose voices have routinely been stifled may become a bigger part of the deliberations—especially for line items that relate to their specific knowledge and expertise. Both of these behavioral changes are constructive and beneficial to better collective decisions and better management teams.

10. *Creating a list of alternatives.*

    This again should be an open process wherein any and all ideas are encouraged. Nothing should be ruled out. In the beginning, these may be very general descriptions about possible directions. They may range from complete and coherent scenarios to bits and pieces. It doesn't matter. The objective is to get all ideas on the table.

11. <u>*Refining alternative scenarios.*</u>

At this point, the objective is to refine alternatives and to be more precise. The bits and pieces can be inserted into larger scenarios or form the beginning of a distinct scenario. Creativity counts. As with individual decisions, the end result will only be as good as the choices that were compared. The range of ideas should come from both inside and outside *the box*. The more alternatives you have the better.

12. <u>*Condensing the number of alternatives.*</u>

There is no correct number of alternatives. Any scenario that might be viable should be left on the board. Any that are obviuisly impractical should be removed. However, any good ideas contained therein should be retained and, if possible, incorporated into the surviving alternatives.

13. <u>*Scoring the first goal.*</u>

Move from top to bottom regardless of where the most important goal(s) are located in the matrix. In fact, it is important to ignore—physically cover them up if necessary—the importance of goal weightings. The relative merit of each alternative in each row should be totally independent of the importance assigned to that goal. Every participant needs to understand this fundamental principle.

Key process note—the isolation of the decision criteria from the assignment of relative merit is one of the primary advantages of this approach. It not only produces better answers but it also changes the way the group works. To wit, the group works *line by line* with no practical way to see how the numbers will add up. It is not a totally blind process as everyone will be aware when they are scoring an important goal. Nevertheless, it is hard to anticipate what the weighted fit will look like until the scoring is finished. Any efforts to distort the scoring will be transparent and not *lost* on the group. Even if there will be some anticipation of results, there will not be answers to view until the same process has been completed for risks. In short, there is no real way to *game* or cheat the system.

Starting with the first row, the group must look over all of the alternatives and agree on which one best fits that particular goal. There may be several that are close. That is fine—the best one will still receive a score of 10 while the others can receive a 9 or less.

Focusing on one line at a time will facilitate agreement. It is dramatically easier to agree on one dimension than it can ever be to agree on the totality of any alternative. The best example probably comes from politics. Consider a bitterly contested presidential election. Even the best of friends can argue vehemently about the candidates with 100% disagreement about the comparative suitability for office. The longer the argument goes the more combative it may become. It is, after all, a winner-take-all proposition. Once a position has been asserted, people rarely retreat or cross over to the other side. However, it would be much easier to get some agreement on specific characteristics and capabilities. For example, who would be more likely to:

- exhibit strong character—honesty, integrity, and courage?
- gain the support of Congress to pass needed legislation?
- be an effective chief executive for a massive bureaucracy?
- connect with, and communicate to, the average citizen?
- become a strong influence on the rest of the world?
- be an effective proponent of economic growth?
- be an effective architect of homeland security?
- be a judicious and respected leader of the military?
- appoint supreme court justices without obvious bias?

I am sure we could modify these and add several more. Some would certainly invite lively debate, but it would be healthy rather than lethal. This would work better than you might expect for two reasons: 1) you can allow your opponents a 10 on any given element without giving up your overall preference and, 2) you are not conceding a 10-point advantage but only the differential—e.g., if your personal preference is assigned a relative score of 7, you have only given up 3 points and that is only for one goal. Agreements will come faster in sequence than is possible when opposing factions are arguing a final choice. The same benefits would accrue to a board of directors choosing a new CEO.

14. *Completing the scoring*.

When all of the goal-fit scoring is completed, the process is repeated for risks. Only then will the group see how the alternatives are shaping up. The results may well be different than expected or different than general discussions would suggest. This is precisely the goal—to find the best weighted fit as opposed to finding the center of a subjective debate. When the results are surprising, it is usually a sign that you are on the path to a better decision.

15. *Reviewing results.*

When one alternative is clearly superior, your work may be finished. If not, the scoring can be reviewed and refined. This can be a fragile moment as biased participants will naturally want to *engineer* a preferred conclusion. Nevertheless, a review at this point may bring up new considerations and a better balance in the numbers. New thoughts will generally suggest minor changes in scoring—e.g., a 7 may become a 6, or a 2 may become a 3. In general, these kinds of refinements will have little effect on the bottom line. If there are substantial changes, they will suggest that the group was somewhat reckless in their initial assessments. In this case, a rational review will become very important to valid results.

Playing "what if" with the scoring is often a more useful approach. This is very easily accomplished with a spreadsheet-driven matrix where the original matrix is saved and then variations in scoring are tested. To the extent that this is an effort to force a favored answer, it will not be valid. However, if testing a range of values for the most subjective elements does not change the answer, the decision will take on added validity. If there is no clear answer, it is time to go back to the list of alternatives and consider more creative scenarios.

16. *Testing the decision.*

Whether or not there appears to be a clear answer, it is usually wise to test the decision for intrinsic merit—comparing it to a standard in the absence of competing alternatives (Chapter IX). This is the only way to assure that you have made a solid decision and not one that is simply better than the other choices considered.

Key process note—I have broken the process down into very small steps so that the logic flow is obvious. In reality, many of these will naturally combine and the process can move smoothly. To ensure an effective flow, it is generally wise to appoint a *discussion or process leader.* It could be the CEO or the most senior executive in attendance, but it is better if the process leader does not have that much sway over the participants. It could be anyone else at the table who is skilled in the process, but it would be best if he or she does not have a functional *axe to grind.*

If possible, I would appoint someone from strategic planning. They will be familiar with all aspects of the business, are likely to be analytical in nature, and are often the most objective regarding functional conflict. If the same process leaders are tapped repeatedly in this fashion, the learning curve will make the process more consistent and more effective for all participants—everyone will know how it works and what to expect.

Key process note—you can add value to the matrix at all stages by recording notes next to each line item. This is beneficial for several reasons.

- It pressures participants to assign scoring on a rational basis.
- It provides a record of why the group assigned specific weightings.
- It improves any subsequent review process if new realities suggest revision.
- It provides critical information to those who may review the matrix independently—in subsequent meetings or when a decision is submitted to upper management.

This last bullet is very important and leads us to the next chapter on selling decisions.

Q: Can this process be integrated with "Six Sigma?"

A: It is a natural fit.

The goal of *Six Sigma* is to improve the efficiency and effectiveness of any business process. It has proven successful in many large companies (most notably General Electric) and continues to grow in popularity. For those who are unfamiliar with it, Six Sigma is a five-step process described by the acronym DMAIC (define, measure, analyze, improve, and control). Step four, "improve", involves the development of alternative solutions and selection of the best path(s). It is here that the decision matrix can dramatically add to the effectiveness of the Six Sigma process—supporting or displacing the "Pay-Off Matrix" as defined by George Eckes (*Six Sigma for Everyone,* John Wiley & Sons, Inc., 2003). It is especially relevant as each decision in Six Sigma is a "group decision" and a critical step in any successful implementation.

Chapter XI

SELLING YOUR DECISIONS

No one operates in a vacuum. From the bottom of every organization to the top, everyone involved in making decisions is also involved in selling them. Specialists and individual contributors will report conclusions and make recommendations to their superiors. High-level executives and officers will do the same in front of presidents and CEOs. Even CEOs report to chairpersons and boards of directors.

It is fine to think of this as the process of *influencing* others, but it is also necessary to be convincing—whether or not you think of it this way, you are *selling* your opinion to others. This holds true for both individual decisions and for group decisions. It is the same issue.

If you have made your decisions based on instinct and *gut feel*, you must then convince others who may not share the same instinct. This challenge is multiplied exponentially when you must convince a group of managers, all with different instincts. If you have made your decisions based on pluses and minuses, you will have the same challenge—others will disagree about the strength and interpretation of your lists. If you use a very complicated decision system, very few will understand it. Those who don't will either attack the process directly or reject the answer *out of hand* to avoid admitting confusion. This is a major limitation with artificial intelligence—everyone wants to know what happened inside the *black box* before they will accept its output. The matrix has the advantages of being both rational and open.

For context, recognize that the process of convincing others is both vertical and horizontal.

The most critical and pressure-packed selling process is upward. For most important decisions, the acceptance, approval and support of higher levels of management is a necessity. It does not matter if you are going as an individual or as a group, the process is the same. It also does not matter if you are *presenting* to an individual manager or an executive review team. The goal is to convince the audience to support your recommendations. In many cases, there will be several meetings as the issue rises within the hierarchy to the level of approval required. Typically, the bigger the price tag, the higher up the chain of command the decision must go. The success of any initiative and perhaps the success of many careers will hang in the balance. How well you can *make your case*—often under pressure—will usually make the difference.

 The second most important selling process is horizontal—convincing others at your same level. These may be other functional leaders who will be needed for support and cooperation. Or, they may simply be important to convincing those above you of the wisdom of a recommended course. In any organization, it is easier to succeed if you have the support of other functions and your own peer group.

The decision matrix as a selling tool. Thus far we have only discussed the use of the matrix as a way to develop and test better decisions. Over the years, I have discovered another hidden quality—the ability to generate support quickly at all levels of management. This is an important dynamic that is universally ignored in discussions of decision theory. However, the best decision in the world won't have much effect if it was turned down.

The ability to sell a good decision is critical to approval and subsequent implementation. The matrix can be a powerful presentation tool in this regard. Just as it can bring together disparate views to make a decision, so also can it generate agreement and support among those with approval and veto powers—even when they have different *agendas* and opinions.

Q: Why is the matrix so effective as a selling tool?

A: Total issue perspective at a glance.

The matrix format and techniques are unique in their ability to compress hundreds of considerations into two simple grids. Consider how much you are presenting when you put up the first goal-fit summary.

- A carefully constructed list of business objectives.
- Identification of the most important goals.
- A weighting of all goals involved in the decision.
- A comprehensive set of alternative actions.
- A detailed expression of relative strengths for each alternative.
- A total weighted fit for each alternative based on a clear set of criteria.

This is a great deal of information on one screen. It displays all aspects of the issues involved as well as the detailed assumptions that support conclusions. The quantification of these assumptions allows every subjective nuance to be an equal part of the equation. Even managers who have never been exposed to the technique should grasp the logic quickly. It can be explained to them in 1-2-3 fashion. The statement might sound like this:

> *"All relevant goals were listed, with the most important assigned a weighting of 10. All other goals were rated in importance relative to this most important one. Each alternative was scored the same way—the best fit was assigned a 10 and all others were rated for relative strength."*

It will be obvious to all how the weighted fit was generated. It is a simple technique. If it were complicated, too much time would be required to explain it and it probably would not be a viable tool for live interaction within a group.

Once participants have seen the goal fit, it is simple to explain how the risk assessment is accomplished—i. e., in the same fashion with 10 used for highest concern and worst case scenario. Be sure to explain that the criteria are different and the numbers are not mathematically comparable—i.e., both sections are valid but are independent of each other.

Key process note—for purposes of clarity, it is beneficial to drop the rule about random sequence for goals and risks. While it is valuable for unbiased scoring, it may be unproductive for presentation purposes. Consider reordering goals and risks from most important to least important. This will provide a more logical structure for presentation purposes and accelerate comprehension. To make the point, I have borrowed an example from Chapter VI and reformatted the criteria in descending order.

Presentation format—Descending goal weights

Alternatives →	WT	Major Marketing Co.		Major Financial Co.	
GOALS	WT	SCORE	PTS	SCORE	PTS
Revenue growth enhancement	10	10	100	5	50
Financial support	9	1	9	10	90
Minimal management effort	8	4	32	10	80
Positive corporate chemistry	7	10	70	4	28
Competitive & industry leverage	7	10	70	7	49
Long term merger potential	3	10	30	3	9
TOTAL (ALL WEIGHTS)	44				
MAXIMUM POSSIBLE POINTS	440	311		306	
% OF MAXIMUM POINTS	100%	71%		70%	

Listing the goals in the order of assigned importance makes the matrix much easier to read. Selective shading helps to distinguish assumptions from mathematical consequences—i.e., the shaded cells are the consequences of assessments displayed in the white cells. The faster the audience understands how the matrix works, the faster it can get past the technique employed and into discussion of results.

Another way to facilitate the process is to include notes that highlight how and why certain alternatives were scored higher than others. These can be shown to the right of the matrix or in a subsequent table underneath. Do not put them first or you will end up discussing alternatives before agreeing on the decision criteria—an obvious step backwards.

If there are disagreements about the criteria employed, it will be beneficial to resolve them up front and to keep them separate from the comparison of alternatives. If you are using a live interactive matrix, suggested revisions of criteria weighting can be quickly tested for bottom-line impact.

In similar fashion, any disagreement regarding relative scoring for alternatives can be tested the same way. It will be obvious whether revisions would produce a material change in the answer. Usually they won't.

If none of the assumptions and weightings is challenged, or if minor revisions have been incorporated, you have established **the foundation for collective agreement.**

Even if the decision is not immediately accepted and top managers want to dwell on the recommendation, you will have the matrix to leave for them to consider. At the very least, you will have demonstrated a rational approach that encompassed all important factors and all visible alternatives. And, you have given them a method—a *lens* through which they can consider the comprehensive aspects of the decision. These results are both preferable to a conventional presentation full of personal perspectives that may fall on deaf ears. Input from senior managers or peer groups should be welcomed—they are more likely to improve the matrix then to stretch it out of balance.

Think of the decision matrix as a summary—*a means of expression*. It may be sufficient to present it alone with assumptive notes, or it may be necessary to provide supporting data and analyses. Either way, the matrix is an effective way to combine all inputs—from subjective thoughts to sophisticated models. Any and all can add to the strength of the matrix and therefore to its conclusions.

The matrix as a summary

Qualitative considerations
Quantitative models
Detailed numerical summaries
Special research studies
Other management input
External consulting input

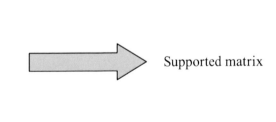 Supported matrix

Backup material will show that you have thought through each aspect and have carefully considered its importance. Either way, a well-thought-out matrix will be a powerful selling tool—how else could you reduce every important aspect of a serious decision to just two numbers: an overall goal fit and risk level? You might find that you, and/or your team, begin to win your cases about 90% of the time.

Chapter XII

THE DECISIVE MANAGEMENT CULTURE

Management time is a scarce resource. How much time do you spend in meetings? How many people are in the room with you and what price tag would you put on the combined investment? It is not just about combined salaries but also about resources and issues left waiting for management attention. Most companies would be shocked by any quantification of this resource drain. Consider also that most high-level meetings spawn a series of *cascading meetings* as the conclusions and directives are passed down through the organization.

Depending on the number and complexity of issues to be addressed, many high-level meetings can easily go all day. Most participants can then spend all or most of the next day just getting the messages and *marching orders* to the next level. Emergency meetings are also common and will disrupt any well-planned calendar. It is easy for a week to disappear into a *sea of meetings.*

At one point in my career, the distraction from meetings was so great that I learned how to multitask—to attend more than one meeting at the same time. Sound impossible? Here are two examples. If I had pressing issues to discuss with my staff, but was scheduled for back-to-back meetings, I would arrange for them to meet me in the hallway at the end of the first meeting. Then, I would hold a 10 to 15 minute meeting with them as we walked through the corridors to my second meeting. If the second meeting started late, I could extent my *hallway meeting* accordingly. This was also an excellent way to make sure my staff was not wasting time waiting for directions that would emanate from my first meeting.

If I had been locked in a long meeting but needed to talk to my staff, I would arrange for them to meet me outside the doorway of my meeting. When the topic ranged into territory that wasn't critical to my function, I would temporarily leave my seat and conduct a meeting in the hallway. Because protocol allowed, I would usually stand in the doorway and quietly hold my meeting while keeping an eye or ear tuned to the primary meeting—I could always rejoin it if necessary. It was just more productive to keep my resources standing in the hallway than to delay critical communications by hours or even a full day.

One of my associates was responsible for important communications to the field sales organization and to factory-scheduling operations. He was constantly writing letters. His problem was that he was always in meetings and never had the time to write. His solution was to dictate letters into a tape recorder during his daily commute—in both directions. His secretary was dismayed each morning as he dropped off two hours of dictation on her desk before heading off to more meetings. Everyone was trying to find more time. One tired executive I know once said he had come to the conclusion that "…his company was in the business of meetings."

As a guest, I once sat through a high-level meeting at a large computer company. At the end of the day, the participants were very satisfied with the meeting while I felt shocked. They were pleased that the meeting had gone well, had been congenial, and had *covered a lot of ground*. In other words, they thought it was a *good meeting*. From my viewpoint, they had spent all day in a friendly and rambling discussion without making any decisions or progress whatsoever. I wondered who was worrying about business results while these senior managers were happily wasting the day. This same meeting would have lasted about 30 minutes at one very large company where I started my career.

The drive for productivity at the management level has a long way to go. Time is critical and is probably the scarcest resource that most managers have—or don't have. Let's face it, meetings are a necessary evil. Whether they are face-to-face or spread over the planet in *virtual* fashion, they are essential for good communications and coordination. If you are going to run a tight ship, everyone will have to know what they are supposed to be doing at all times. The challenge is to find a consistent way to shorten meetings without sacrificing effectiveness.

Two forces are at work—issue complexity and management style. While I wouldn't suggest it as a panacea, the decision matrix can address both forces and can dramatically impact management productivity. If it is used in an interactive way to develop a consensus, it may save from 25% to 50% in meeting time. If completed prior to the meeting and then used as a method of presentation and refinement, it may save up to 80% in meeting time. In my experience, it is not unusual for a meeting that might have lasted for several hours to be over in 15 to 30 minutes—that is the potential power of compressing all aspects of a complicated decision into one simple graphic supported by the matrix. Think about what you might do with a few extra hours each week.

Better results. Nothing in this text is meant to suggest that the quality of decisions should be compromised for the sake of speed. On the contrary, the primary objective is to make the best possible decisions. It was only by accident that I discovered how effective the matrix could be in building a consensus and building it quickly. I didn't set out to shorten meetings but only to communicate the thought process that supported my decisions and recommendations. The reduction in the amount of time needed to resolve an issue was a surprising but consistent by-product.

Everyone knows how expensive mistakes can be. Most important decisions involve financial, physical, and human resources and the global marketplace is not a forgiving environment—lost time and opportunities are hard to recover. Making better decisions the first time always produces better results and produces them sooner.

The potential of a more decisive culture. Perhaps you will be the only person using this technique in your company. Perhaps you will use it sparingly, only for critical issues. Even if this is the case, the matrix should serve you well. You will easily distinguish problems from decisions and will not mix objectives with the alternative means to achieve them. Those around and above you should quickly learn to appreciate the logic with which you present your arguments. You will also move faster and with more confidence. Asking your subordinates to use it will also improve the quality of recommendations coming up to you for approval.

But what if many managers and executives adopted this approach? What would happen if it spread throughout a corporate culture? Then something remarkable might happen. Not only might management teams begin to *think* about decisions in the same way, but they might begin to *communicate* assumptions and decisions in the same manner—using the matrix as a common means of expression. This would compress communications while increasing the rate at which information is absorbed. The net effects could be better decisions and better results while the organization moves faster—producing an overall **acceleration of the management process**.

In most organizations, there is a natural set of barriers that prevent this kind of collective productivity. Chief among these is the fact that each manager has his or her own approach to decisions. This is closely followed by personal opinion, functional bias, and political alignment. When these are spread over large numbers of participants and complex issues, the entire process is sluggish, burdensome, and often produces sub-optimal results. The matrix may or may not become popular in your company. However, to the extent that it is adopted, new possibilities are created. A consistent and rational approach can begin to knock down the barriers that have always hindered productivity at the executive level. Less time will be wasted and the business should be able to steer a finer course through the challenges of modern business.

It is not difficult to test this potential. All that is necessary is to apply the principles set forth in this book to one decision, just as I did 35 years ago. You will have one big advantage—a process refined by application to thousands of decisions over several decades. **Aim for 90%** and see what happens.

Appendix A

Instructions—Using a Matrix Library[*]

Media: While you can use a blackboard, flip chart, or pad of paper to build a decision matrix, the most productive medium is the spreadsheet. It is strongly recommended for its speed, flexibility, and interactive capabilities. Whether you are making a decision by yourself or acting in a group, the spreadsheet is ideal for the insertion of new ideas, the refinement of assumptions, color coding, and the testing of preliminary answers.

Format: In any corporate environment, it will be helpful to develop standard formats. Consistency in terms of colors and layout will help everyone read the matrix faster and understand its output. For example, in all of my formats, the clear or white cells are intended for input while the shaded cells are pre-programmed for calculations and graphics—they are fixed in function. Also, standard and distinct colors should be established for goal and risk sections. This will accelerate understanding by all reviewers and will serve to make graphic summaries instantly meaningful without explanation.

Matrix library: To facilitate repeated use, it is helpful to have a library of pre-programmed blank matrices. These should be constructed to accommodate decisions of various dimensions—e.g., two to ten columns for alternatives and five to ten rows each for goals and risks.

Guidelines for use:

1. Picking the right matrix—look at the number of alternatives you are considering and the approximate number of goals and risks you have identified. Choose a matrix that is larger than you think you will need—you can always eliminate columns and rows later without affecting calculations or graphics.

2. Important—save the chosen matrix with your own file name before you enter any information. This will protect the blank matrix from corruption and make it much easier to use the next time. It

also means you can start over easily if you make a mistake or see the need for a larger or smaller matrix.

3. Color coding—it is usually best to choose conservative colors for shaded cells and graphics. This will make the formats more appropriate for a broad corporate audience and a variety of circumstances. Conservative colors will also be less likely to visually distract viewers from content.

4. Group interaction—when entering data in a live, interactive session, be careful not to accidentally enter data in the shaded cells; you do not want your audience to wait while you restore the cell's functionality. The best approach is to "protect" the shaded cells (where calculations are completed) to make sure the matrix is not corrupted.

5. Creating a benchmark test format—after saving the completed matrix, save it again with a separate file name. Then merely delete the columns for the weaker alternatives until only the preferred choice is left. Leave the "weights" unchanged but delete the "scoring" for that alternative as you will be re-scoring for intrinsic merit (see Chapter IX or Appendix B). You may also want to delete the graph as it will be of little use and will create space for relevant notes.

6. Expertise—any one with simple skills in the use of Microsoft Excel should be able to construct and manage a library of electronic matrix blanks with little effort.

---

* Note: readers are invited to visit www.tpmcauliffe.com for access to pre-programmed, interactive matrix examples that can be downloaded freely for personal and corporate use.

Appendix B

Instructions—Decision Matrix Basics

Process for goals and objectives

1. Enter your list in random order. This will help to keep bias out of our weighting and scoring. Expand your list to make sure that all important goals are included.

2. Condense the list to make it more compact and therefore easier to assign weights. Eliminate duplications and combine similar items as excessive numbers of items will tend to distort results. Avoid unimportant elements as they will dilute your more important considerations.

3. Weight your list carefully—always begin by assigning a 10 to the most important goal. You may only use 10 once.

4. Scoring all others—start at the top of the list and go line by line. Compare each item separately to the most important factor—the one that received the 10. Do not compare these items to each other at this point but only to the goal with a 10. Give each a weight of from 1 to 9. You can use any of these as many times as you want—this is not a forced ranking (e.g., in theory, each of these could receive a 5).

5. Double checking—when all goals have been weighted, go back to see how each item on your list is weighted compared to all others. Adjust the weightings to make sure more important items are differentiated from those of lesser importance. Also make sure that moderately important items are not over-weighted.

6. Scoring alternatives—start with the first goal on your list. Work from top to bottom. Do not jump ahead.

7. Objectivity—completely ignore the weightings you have assigned to your goals. Any consideration of these at this stage might bias your scoring and undermine the validity of results.

8. Strongest fit—look across the alternatives in each row. Find the one that best fits that specific goal and assign it a 10. Even if some are nearly identical, there is always one that will be the best.

9. Relative fit—now rate all other alternatives relative to the 10 assigned to the best fit. This is essentially the same as the process you used to assign weights to goals. The primary difference is that you are now working horizontally across the matrix, one line at a time. Do not look at how alternatives have scored against other goals—stay focused on one goal at a time. A second difference is that you can use 0 (zero) in those rare cases where it is a more accurate measure than 1.

10. Weighted fit—when you have finished all scoring, multiply goal weights by relative scoring for alternatives and add them for a measure of overall fit.

11. Percentage fit—convert the summary points for each alternative and compare them to the maximum possible points (total of all goal weights x 10). The resulting percentages will facilitate quick interpretation of comparative strength versus your criteria.

Process for risks and negative potential

1. List of risks—create this list just as you created your list of goals and objectives above. Keep them in random order. Be expansive to make sure all potential negatives are included and then compress the list by eliminating duplications.

2. Weighting—the weighting process is the same. Find the most serious risk and assign it a 10. Assign 1-9 to the remaining items based on their relative seriousness.

3. Scoring of alternatives—just as with goals, find the alternative with the highest risk and assign it a 10. Assign 0-9 to the others so that those of lowest risk receive the lowest score—e.g., very low risk would be a 1, 2, or 3. Do not over-weight risks of moderate to low importance as you will dilute the influence of your most significant concerns.

4. Weighted fit—the multiplication and addition process mirrors that for goals and objectives. The alternative(s) with the highest totals are those with the highest levels of risk or negative potential.

5. Percentage fit—convert the summary points for each alternative and compare it to the maximum possible points (total of all risk weights x 10). The resulting percentages will facilitate quick interpretation.

Interpretation

Evaluating results is straightforward. Numerical totals and graphic representations show the degree to which each alternative fits your criteria. Keep in mind that positive fit (*vis-à-vis* goals) is only directly comparable from one alternative to another. Because negative fit (risk) is based on a different set of criteria, these totals are only comparable mathematically from one alternative to another.

Using the percentages of maximum potential will facilitate interpretations for each decision and also serve to establish consistent benchmarks and commonality for review of ongoing decisions.

See Appendix C—Advanced Techniques & Reminders for additional refinements.

Appendix C

Advanced Techniques & Reminders

The following is a comprehensive list of advanced matrix techniques extracted from the book. If you are approaching a serious decision, you might want to review this appendix before getting started. While it will not guarantee a perfect answer, it will certainly improve your chances of finding one.

1. Develop your decision criteria before beginning any consideration of potential alternatives. If you allow consideration of alternatives, even in nascent forms, you may inadvertently influence and undermine the validity of your criteria.

2. For purposes of unbiased scoring, keep your goals and risks in random order. Any other sequence can influence the objectivity of your results. For purposes of executive presentation, eliminate this rule and present all criteria in order of most to least important (see number 15 below). The sequence for alternatives should be random in both cases and will not impact scoring validity or speed of interpretation.

3. Goals should represent positive outcomes. Risks should reflect negative outcomes. Resist the temptation to make the "avoidance of a negative" into a goal. Conversely, you may wish to show the "failure to reach a goal" as a risk. This will not undermine the mathematical integrity of your answers but should be used selectively—your risk criteria should not look like the mirror image of your goal criteria.

4. Always distinguish and account for the reversibility factor. Any decision that is hard to reverse or "undo" should be elevated in importance to reflect this risk.

5. Make sure you have not left out any goals or risks that are not obvious but might be important. Don't be surprised later by a goal or risk you failed to consider.

6. Number 5 above notwithstanding, compress your lists of goals and risks as much as possible. Do not inadvertently include any duplicates—they will dilute the value of your most important considerations and thereby distort your results.

7. Do not overrate the importance of too many goals or risks—doing this will dilute consideration of your most important factors and undermine the validity of your answers. Differentiate: force yourself to give much lower ratings to less-important or secondary factors. To test how well you have done this, look at the range of weightings between the most and least important. If there is nothing lower than 6 or 7, you should review your numbers carefully. Also check to see what percentage the most important goal (and risk) represents of the total criteria. For example:

Total criteria points	Value of 10 (most important)
100	10%
65	15%
50	20%
40	25%

Adjust your criteria until the "influences" of your most important goals and risks are properly reflected.

8. Be creative with your development of alternatives. Make sure the best option has a chance to compete with more conservative or conventional ideas. You may find some better options by combining pieces of alternatives or adding elements from outside the box. Your decision can only be optimal if the best possible choice is considered.

9. There is no limit to the number of alternatives you may consider. Often it is necessary to start with an expansive number and then condense the list; eliminating the weaker choices with each step. Recognize that each time you condense the list, you must re-score the relative strength of each alternative. The goal and risk criteria should not change. Notice also that, as you squeeze the number of alternatives, the 10-point rule will shift risks from weaker alternatives to those remaining. The effect should be minor for goal-fit comparisons (stronger to start with) but may be dramatic for risks. Do not be

concerned about this dynamic—it is a mathematical certainty. You are still looking for the best among several choices and can, in the end, test the winner for intrinsic merit as described in Chapter IX.

10. If your best alternative does not pass the intrinsic merit test, it is a signal that none of your defined options is good enough and that you need to be more creative. You can look for ways to strengthen the best choice, find new alternatives, or both. Doing both will often put you on the path to an optimal decision.

11. Do not cheat on yourself. There are several ways you can compromise your results—avoid the following:

    - Looking ahead to see how the answer (point totals) are shaping up.
    - Looking at criteria weightings while comparing alternatives. You may be tempted to *engineer* your answers—i.e., making your favorite alternatives score well versus the most important goals.
    - Looking at the final goal-fit results (on top) while scoring risks (below). This will tempt you to give lower risk scores to your preferred alternatives. Always ensure that *goal scoring* remains completely independent from *risk scoring*. They are only combined in the end. Premature comparisons can undermine the integrity of your answers.
    - Playing *what if* to see how the answers may change with minor adjustments in criteria weighting or alternative scoring. You might do this to test for answer "sensitivity" but be careful not to *force* answers in this way.

12. Always keep records of your results. They may be important to future deliberations. If the world changes or new ideas surface, a saved matrix will provide an easy way to reflect an updated picture. Here are several examples:

    - Revising your criteria with better knowledge—adding important new factors or eliminating lesser considerations.
    - Adding new or more creative alternatives while eliminating weaker options.
    - Keeping existing alternatives but finding ways to make them better.
    - Updating weightings for goals and risks based on new company priorities.

- Running a quick test on a new decision that closely resembles one from the past.
- Running a test for intrinsic merit for a choice that was only measured against other leading alternatives.

13. It is always a good idea to test answers for intrinsic merit. Determining an adequate score will depend on the significance of the decision and the Company's tolerance for mediocrity. A strong goal fit will normally fall in the 85% to 90% range. Any alternative scoring more than 90% should be very solid. A reasonable level of risk will normally fall in the 25% range but may be lower for very good choices. 10% (all factors x 1) is the practical minimum score for risks. Therefore, any alternative at 15% or less should be considered very low risk. Certain patterns and standard benchmarks should become apparent with minimal experience.

14. When approaching a group decision, make sure to control the discussion in the following manner.

- Establish lists of goals and risks before any discussion of alternatives.
- Compress and weight the value of all goals and risks before discussing any alternatives.
- Press for creative alternatives to measure against more traditional and conservative notions.
- Score relative fit for each alternative on a line by line basis—do not jump around the matrix or look ahead to answers.
- Be prepared to test ranges of scoring. Make sure this is done objectively—do not let participants contort the matrix to produce a desired answer.
- Consider using a "discussion leader" who does not have a functional bias or too much authority but is respected by the entire group.

15. When selling or communicating a completed matrix, always re-order goals and risks so that they are in descending order of importance. This will greatly enhance high-speed interpretation. Also include notes so that primary scoring assumptions are made clear to recipients. These two actions will reduce the number of questions prompted and accelerate a productive discussion of results.

Appendix D

Decision Worksheets

ISSUE: _____

ALTERNATIVES ⇨										
GOALS	WT	SCORE	PTS	SCORE	PTS	SCORE	PTS	SCORE	PTS	SCORE	PTS
TOTAL – WEIGHTS		(NOT APPLICABLE – LEAVE BLANK)									
TOTAL – POINTS	NA	⇨		⇨		⇨		⇨		⇨	
% REL. GOAL FIT	NA										

RISKS	WT	SCORE	PTS	SCORE	PTS	SCORE	PTS	SCORE	PTS	SCORE	PTS
TOTAL – WEIGHTS		(NOT APPLICABLE – LEAVE BLANK)									
TOTAL – POINTS	NA	⇨		⇨		⇨		⇨		⇨	
% REL. RISK LEVEL	NA										

For an interactive, color-coded version of this matrix with automated graphics (in Microsoft Excel ® 2003) go to www.tpmcauliffe.com. Do not use without thorough review of instructions and optimization techniques. Use this form for initial decision considerations and rough drafts.

ISSUE: _____

ALTERNATIVES ⇨										
GOALS	WT	SCORE	PTS	SCORE	PTS	SCORE	PTS	SCORE	PTS	SCORE	PTS
TOTAL – WEIGHTS		(NOT APPLICABLE – LEAVE BLANK)								
TOTAL – POINTS	NA	⇨		⇨		⇨		⇨		⇨	
% REL. GOAL FIT	NA										

RISKS	WT	SCORE	PTS	SCORE	PTS	SCORE	PTS	SCORE	PTS	SCORE	PTS
TOTAL – WEIGHTS		(NOT APPLICABLE – LEAVE BLANK)								
TOTAL – POINTS	NA	⇨		⇨		⇨		⇨		⇨	
% REL. RISK LEVEL	NA										

For an interactive, color-coded version of this matrix with automated graphics (in Microsoft Excel ® 2003) go to www.tpmcauliffe.com. Do not use without thorough review of instructions and optimization techniques. Use this form for initial decision considerations and rough drafts.